Contents

S0-AWI-638

Nina's address book

ANTIQUES

B + T ANTIQUES
47 Ledbury Road
London W11 2AA
+44 (0)20 7229 7001
www.bntantiques.co.uk

BIRGIT ISRAEL
301 Fulham Road
London SW10 9QH
+44 (0)20 7376 7255
www.birgitisrael.com

CARLTON DAVIDSON
507 Kings Road
London SW10 0TX
+44 (0)20 7795 0905

GUINEVERE ANTIQUES
574–580 Kings Road
London SW6 2DY
+44 (0)20 7736 2917
www.guinevere.co.uk

BATHROOMS

BATHROOMS INTERNATIONAL
4 Pont Street
London SW1X 9EL
+44 (0)20 7838 7788
www.bathroomsint.com

CARPETS AND RUGS

PARSUA
Fairbank Studios 2
65-69 Lots Road
London SW10 0RN
+44 (0)20 7351 6111
www.cb-parsua.com

STARK CARPET
3rd Floor, South Dome
Chelsea Harbour
Design Centre
Chelsea Harbour
London SW10 0XE
+44 (0)20 7352 6001
www.starkcarpet.com

CURTAIN FITTINGS

McKINNEY AND CO
Studio P
The Old Imperial Laundry
71 Warriner Gardens
London SW11 4XW
+44 (0)20 7627 5077

FABRICS

CLAREMONT
35 Elystan Street
London SW3 3NT
+44 (0)20 7581 9575
www.claremontfurnishing.com

LELIÈVRE
108–110 Chelsea Harbour
Design Centre
Chelsea Harbour
London SW10 0XE
+44 (0)20 7352 4798
www.lelievre.co.uk

PIERRE FREY
251-253 Fulham Road
London SW3 6HY
+44 (0)20 7376 5599
www.pierrefrey.com

SAHCO HESSLEIN
G24 Chelsea Harbour
Design Centre
Chelsea Harbour
London SW10 0XE
+44 (0)20 7352 6168
www.sahco-hesslein.com

TISSUS D'HÉLÈNE
421 The Chambers
Chelsea Harbour
London SW10 0XF
+44 (0) 20 7352 9977

ZIMMER & ROHDE
15 Chelsea Harbour
Design Centre
Chelsea Harbour
London SW10 0XE
+44 (0)20 7351 7115

FLOORING

AA FLOORING
24 Howard Close Business Park
Waltham Abbey
Essex EN9 1XE
England
+44 (0)1992 769100

ELEMENT 7
Unit 2
Parsons Green Depot
Parsons Green Lane
London SW6 4HH
+44 (0)20 7736 2366
www.element7.co.uk

FURNITURE AND FURNITURE MAKING

BEN WHISTLER
33 The Arches
Broughton Street
London SW8 3QR
+44 (0)20 7622 6246
www.benwhistler.com

CHRISTOPHER CLARK
Sovereign Way
Trafalgar Industrial Estate
Downham Market
Norfolk PE38 9SW
England
+44 (0)1366 389400
www.christopherclark.co.uk

JULIA GRAY
D&D Building
979 3rd Avenue
New York, NY 10022
+1 (0)212 223 4454

NINA CAMPBELL

DECORATING

Journal

CICO BOOKS

LONDON NEW YORK

Published in 2008 by CICO Books
an imprint of Ryland, Peters & Small Ltd

20–21 Jockey's Fields, London WC1R 4BW
519 Broadway, 5th Floor, New York NY 10012

10 9 8 7 6 5 4 3 2 1

A CIP catalogue record for this book is
available from the Library of Congresss
and the British Library.

UK ISBN-13: 978 1 906094 53 9
US ISBN-13: 978 1 906094 54 6

Printed in China

Editor Alison Wormleighton
Designer Roger Hammond
Style photography Jan Baldwin, Paul Ryan, Tim
Beddow, Christopher Drake, Douglas Friedman
and Philip Ennis

Niermann Weeks
60 Generals Highway
Millersville
MD 21108
USA
+1 (0)410 923 0123
www.niermannweeks.com

Parson's Table
362 Fulham Road
London SW10 9UU
+44 (0)20 7352 7444

William Yeoward
270 Kings Road
London SW3 5AW
+44 (0)20 7349 7828
www.williamyeoward.com

GARDEN FURNITURE
McKinnon and Harris
PO Box 4885
Richmond
Virginia 23220-1109
USA
+1 (0)804 358 2385
www.mckinnonandharris.com

KITCHENS
Kitchen Central
19 Carnwath Road
London SW6 3EN
+44 (0)20 7736 6458
www.kitchencentral.co.uk

LIGHTING
David Butler
31 Richmond Way
London W14 OAS
+44 (0)20 7603 2254

Forbes and Lomax
205a St Johns Hill
London SW11 1TH
+44 (0)20 7738 0202
www.forbesandlomax.co.uk

Lucy Cope
Foxhill House
Allington
Chippenham
Wiltshire SN14 6LL
England
+44 (0)1249 650446
www.lucycope.com

LINEN
Monogrammed Linen Shop
168 Walton Street
London SW3 3JL
+44 (0)20 7589 4033
www.monogrammedlinenshop.com

PAINTING, SPECIALIST PAINTING, DECORATING
Catherine Cummings
49 Sydney Street
London SW3 6PX
+44 (0)20 7306 2670

Hallmark Decor
32 Thames Street
Canvey Island
Essex SS8 0HH
England
+44 (0)1268 696913

John Sumpter
82 Overstone Road
London W6 OAB
+44 (0)20 8748 0992

PICTURE FRAMING AND RESTORATION
Campbell's of London
33 Thurloe Place
London SW7 2HQ
+44 (0) 20 7584 9268
www.campbellsoflondon.co.uk

PICTURE HANGING
Phoenix Fine Art
15 Mayday Gardens
London SE3 8NJ
+44 (0)20 8319 3527

ROCK CRYSTAL LOGS
Ruzzetti and Gow
3rd floor
22 East 72nd Street
New York, NY 10021
+1 (0)212 327 4281
www.ruzzettiandgow.com

WINDOW TREATMENTS, UPHOLSTERY, WALLING
Bray Design
Units 1 + 5
Hawes Hill Farm
Drift Road
Winkfield
Berkshire SL4 4QQ
England
+44 (0)1344 890998

Edge Interiors
8 Clarendon Terrace
London W9 1BZ
+44 (0)20 7289 1189
www.edgeinteriors.co.uk

Garvey Brothers
39 The Baulk
London SW18 5RA
+44 (0)20 8871 1739

J & B Contracts
2A Denbigh Place
London SW1V 2HB
England
+44 (0)20 7622 4614

Len Carter
37 Shuttleworth Road
London SW11 3DH
England
+44 (0)20 7228 6676

Favourite suppliers

Use these pages to record suppliers such as curtain makers, slipcover makers, carpet layers, hard-flooring suppliers, picture framers, plumbers, electricians, builders, architects and decorators you have used or have had recommended to you.

Name _____

Address _____
_____
_____

Tel _____

Fax _____

Email _____

www. _____

Speciality _____

Association of which a member _____
_____

Comments _____
_____
_____

Name _____

Address _____
_____
_____

Tel _____

Fax _____

Email _____

www. _____

Speciality _____

Association of which a member _____
_____

Comments _____
_____
_____

Name _____

Address _____
_____
_____

Tel _____

Fax _____

Email _____

www. _____

Speciality _____

Association of which a member _____
_____

Comments _____
_____
_____

Name _____

Address _____
_____
_____

Tel _____

Fax _____

Email _____

www. _____

Speciality _____

Association of which a member _____
_____

Comments _____
_____
_____

Name

Address

Tel

Fax

Email

www.

Speciality

Association of which a member

Comments

Name

Address

Tel

Fax

Email

www.

Speciality

Association of which a member

Comments

Name

Address

Tel

Fax

Email

www.

Speciality

Association of which a member

Comments

Name

Address

Tel

Fax

Email

www.

Speciality

Association of which a member

Comments

Name _____

Address _____

_____

_____

_____

Tel _____

Fax _____

Email _____

www. _____

Speciality _____

Association of which a member _____

_____

Comments _____

_____

_____

_____

Name _____

Address _____

_____

_____

_____

Tel _____

Fax _____

Email _____

www. _____

Speciality _____

Association of which a member _____

_____

Comments _____

_____

_____

_____

Name _____

Address _____

_____

_____

_____

Tel _____

Fax _____

Email _____

www. _____

Speciality _____

Association of which a member _____

_____

Comments _____

_____

_____

_____

Name _____

Address _____

_____

_____

_____

Tel _____

Fax _____

Email _____

www. _____

Speciality _____

Association of which a member _____

_____

Comments _____

_____

_____

_____

Favourite interiors websites

www. _____

Notes _____

_____

_____

www. _____

Notes _____

_____

_____

www. _____

Notes _____

_____

_____

www. _____

Notes _____

_____

_____

www. _____

Notes _____

_____

_____

www. _____

Notes _____

_____

_____

www. _____

Notes _____

_____

_____

www. _____

Notes _____

_____

_____

www. _____

Notes _____

_____

_____

www. _____

Notes _____

_____

_____

www. _____

Notes _____

_____

_____

www. _____

Notes _____

_____

_____

Elements of design

Styles in decorating come and go, but my philosophy has always been pretty consistent. My personal taste is for a house that is glamorous, comfortable and easy to live in and reflects the lifestyle and personality of the owner. But I do not live in the past. Today's technologies give the designer an unbelievable amount of scope, and houses can be warmer, cooler, lighter and brighter than they ever were.

Building up the layers

Interior design allows you to combine many elements – fabrics, papers, paints, flooring, furniture and accessories – to produce whatever look you want for your home. Think of a room as having many layers, each of which needs to play its part in the overall effect, from the large elements, such as sofas and windows, to the smallest candle shade or pillow. The trick is not to think about these things in isolation, but to consider how each ingredient works with the others to build up a look that is both visually stunning and absolutely practical.

All too often people rush to the fun part, such as choosing paint colours and fabric swatches, but there is a whole layer of important decisions that must be taken first. If a home is not

ABOVE: *All the elements of a room are interdependent – they work together to create the total effect. Choose them with this in mind but do not be afraid to try unusual combinations that appeal to you.*

practical, then it is not going to be comfortable and you will always be irritated by it. So do not get distracted by detail or start choosing individual items, such as carpets or sofas, until you have established what your design brief is – your aims, priorities, restrictions. Never sacrifice comfort and functionality to aesthetics. Once the space makes sense and the bones of your scheme are in place, then is the time to think about creating the atmosphere you have in mind and delight in beautifully crafted details of design, from inlaid furniture to handmade trimmings.

Comfort is at the heart of my style.

Suit yourself

Begin by thinking about the layout, the flow of space and the functions and requirements of each area; this should help you plan any plumbing or electrical work that needs to be done. Decisions also have to be made at the beginning if you are changing the lighting (see pages 16–19) or heating system, moving radiators or installing a music system, air conditioning or a security system, for example. Draw up a master plan setting out your priorities (see page 29).

Be prepared to edit some of your possessions in order to achieve the look you desire. Very often decorating is not so much about adding in the new, as taking out some of the old. Try to look at your surroundings with a fresh eye and keep your mind open to the many different possibilities a room offers. Making compromises is not always a bad thing; in fact, it can ignite some clever ideas.

ABOVE AND RIGHT: *Identifying priorities at the beginning of a project will help ensure that the design of a room suits your needs. In this living/dining room where space is at a premium, radiator covers beneath the windows create useful window seats, while roman blinds (shades) take up less space than curtains.*

Where to begin

The first step is to study the basic shell of a room and consider all its potential. You have to train the eye, so that no matter how unpromising the existing decor is, you can look around and imagine everything stripped away, with only the skeleton remaining. For most people, the hardest part of decorating is combining function – the uses a room has – with the space available. The secret is to pay as much attention to unglamorous issues, such as storage, as you might to choosing flooring or a curtain fabric.

The aim is to end up with a space that will work for you. Try to keep your mind as open as possible and to look beyond the room's obvious uses. These days, living rooms often have to double as spare bedrooms, kitchens as family sitting rooms, dining rooms as studies, and bedrooms as gymnasiums. Go through the questionnaire in the relevant chapter and draw up a list showing who uses the room and for what. Begin to consider how the room breaks down into zones and various tasks. What is important is to use all the available space.

Making sense of the space

When assessing the possibilities of a room, you need to study it from all angles. Measure the dimensions, noting the width of each wall and the ceiling height on a floor plan (see pages 32–3). Consider the proportions of the room, including its shape and height and the width and position of doors and windows. It is rare to find a space that is perfect in every way; nearly always there are modifications that could be made.

Structural changes

Perhaps the ceiling is too low, the windows are too narrow, the doors open the wrong way, the natural light is poor or the rooms are simply too small. Don't be afraid of reducing the value of a property by reducing the number of rooms – if the result looks and works better, you won't.

ABOVE: *Structural changes can make a huge improvement. Here we created new, outsized doorways and framed them with mirrored architraves.*

Creating a sense of space doesn't have to involve knocking down walls, however. Think about what you could achieve simply by borrowing space to

make cupboards or by moving or enlarging doors. You can turn windows into doors or doors into windows. Obviously with all these changes there may be regulations to follow or structural issues, so these are not do-it-yourself jobs. Drastic measures may be necessary if you are to achieve the look you want.

Architectural details

Architectural features are a boon, but they should not interfere with how well a space works on a practical level. Look at the room's particular features – do skirting boards (baseboards), picture rails, doors and door frames, a fireplace or other integral parts of the room suit its style? It could

ABOVE AND OPPOSITE: *This sitting room had previously been formed by knocking two small rooms together, but each still had its own doorway. We bricked up one doorway, creating enough wall space for a decent-sized sofa, added a door to the garden and introduced a second fireplace at the other end so the room was more balanced.*

be that they have been added on at some later date and look completely incongruous. The architectural finish matters and is much more noticeable than you would think, particularly in a small room.

One of the challenges of modern houses and apartments is a lack of architectural detail. It can be added but needs to be done with sensitivity.

I often commission extra architectural detail.

Rather than adding a pastiche of inappropriate period elements, however, you could take one magnificent architectural detail or antique work of art and use it as the inspiration for a theme throughout.

Finding solutions

The next step is to look at ways of solving some of these problems. Quite often making doors wider and taller can add a greater sense of scale to a space. Perhaps there are structural alterations that would help – such as knocking through to an adjacent space, removing bulky closets or built-in cupboards or introducing a decorative moulding of some sort. If these decisions are beyond your budget, don't despair – decorating a room well can mask many of its faults.

Whatever the size of your home, it is essential to think about your storage requirements, to prevent the rooms from looking cluttered and chaotic. The golden rule here is that everything you possess must have a home within your home – and that you must be disciplined enough to put things away. You can never have enough storage, so plan this in as early as possible in the interior design process.

Effective lighting

Never underestimate the importance of light – both natural and artificial – in a room. Light is one of those life-enhancing ingredients that are always worth spending time and money on to get just right. Even when you are working on a tight budget, a well thought-out lighting scheme should be at the top of your list of priorities – it will always update a room and improve the atmosphere. So many other things in the room, including furniture and fabrics, can be upgraded in the future if need be. But once the walls are finished, it is too late to wish you had invested in more sympathetic lighting.

Looking at light

Lighting plays many tricks and not all of them are kind. Dull, flat lighting is not just unflattering, it will also dampen your spirits. By contrast, a well-lit (and that does not necessarily equate with bright) room will make you feel happier and more alert.

First study the natural light available – not only the size and number of windows, but also the quality of light coming into the home and how it changes according to the time of day.

ABOVE AND OPPOSITE: *Well-planned lighting makes a huge difference to a room. The strategically placed standard lamps in the drawing room above provide good reading light as well as a warm glow. In the dining room opposite, the impact of the massed candles has been doubled by placing them in front of a large mirror.*

Artificial lighting isn't just there for evening and night-time use; it is often an essential for boosting daylight, too. You must have an awareness of when the room is at its best and worst in terms of light.

This is not simply on a day-to-day basis, but also season to season, because natural light changes dramatically through the year.

Types of lighting

Now go back to the list of functions you drew up (see page 12). Task lighting is what makes the difference between a poorly lit and a well-lit room. If you always like to read in the same armchair, you need a lamp behind your shoulder that throws light onto the page without dazzling you. If you have a desk at which you write letters, you need a lamp by your side that will cast its beam onto the paper. This idea continues throughout your home, according to the functions of each room.

If you have a particularly fine painting or collection of crystals, say, it makes sense to light it to its best advantage. Clever use of accent lighting like this can add to the drama of the room.

But that is not all. There is another layer of light – ambient, or background lighting – that is equally important. This is what brings a feel-good factor to a room, and it is also what allows you to alter the mood instantly. Controllability is important, so make sure that lamps can all be centrally operated. You should be able to walk into your home and flick a switch that controls all the lamps on a ring circuit, rather than walking from room to room switching on each one individually. Always install more power sockets (outlets) than you think you need so that you have the flexibility to move lamps around.

OPPOSITE AND RIGHT: *Use lighting to create a particular atmosphere. The panelled room shown opposite is lit only by standard lamps with marbled-paper shades and by picture lights for a cosy effect. In the dining room on the right, gilt sconces are installed on some of the mirror panels around the room, reflecting the soft glow from the French candle bulbs.*

Tip
Sockets (outlets) set into the floor near tables prevent trailing electric leads.

Creating atmosphere

Avoid relying heavily on a central ceiling light, as it can flatten and dull a room, rather than bringing it to life as good lighting should do. If you have a period house, do not feel that dreary pendant lighting is somehow traditional. Most historic houses were not built to have electric light anyway. Discreet halogen spots inset into the ceiling to highlight pictures and architectural details, combined with candlelight, can create an effect closer to the original than pendant lighting.

Candles are a simple form of ambient lighting, as they cast such a romantic and sympathetic glow. Do not be restricted to using them on the table – floor-standing holders and wall sconces allow more opportunities. Make more of them by placing them against reflective surfaces, such as mirror.

Style decisions

Once you have got the basics of the room right, you can allow yourself to think about style and decorating. The architectural style of the house is obviously a factor here – it should not necessarily dictate how you decorate a room, but add another layer of inspiration.

Old and new

If you move into a modern house in any part of the world, spend a little time looking at the traditions of the area. You don't have to turn your home into a pastiche, but local designs will probably look better than incorporating inappropriate French fireplaces or the latest fashion. Crisp, modern design and antiques can complement each other beautifully, and mixing the two creates a home full of personality.

ABOVE AND OPPOSITE: *Do not be afraid to mix antique and modern. In my previous apartment (above) an antique silver coffee service had a contemporary setting, and in my present house (opposite) a black lacquer Biedermeier chest rubs shoulders with modern art and furniture.*

When you have a beautiful historic room to start with, boasting lots of period detail and high ceilings, you have to achieve a harmonious balance between old and new. Contemporary, in the context of a period house, means respecting period detail and treating it simply, then keeping fabrics, artwork and other details unfussy.

Visual impact

Think about the view from one room into another. Walk around the room you are planning to decorate, thinking about the traffic routes from one area to another and what you would see from each point. Consider what you would notice if you were walking in for the first time – immediate dramatic impact is important. Remember to take into account eye levels when sitting as well as when standing, so that there is something to catch the eye at all times.

Harmony and unity

Homes should have a thread running through them, linking each space with the next. It can jar the nerves if there is too much of a jump aesthetically from one space to another. You don't have to repeat schemes, but rather try to pick out themes within them that can be carried through to the next room. A rug, for example, can set the standard for the range of colours to be used around it; or you might take the colours from one room and use them in a different configuration in the next. The idea is to achieve a sense of balance – you do not want anything that jostles for attention or detracts from the feeling of calm.

This is particularly important in a small home. Creating harmony and unity throughout the house – perhaps even by keeping the carpet or flooring the same and the colours neutral – makes the rooms appear larger than they really are. In a large home, however, you can afford to have dramatic contrast between rooms, provided they are linked in some way.

When rooms all flow into each other to form one huge open-plan space, a unified approach to colour and style is vital. You can still give each area a strong visual identity of its own. Choose a basic palette consisting of two – or at most three – harmonious colours.

I love to combine classic and contemporary.

Using pattern and colour

This is the part that everyone loves but that also causes the biggest headaches. Not only can it be disappointing to find that the fabric swatch you ordered with such optimism does not look quite as you intended, but it is also an expensive mistake if you get it wrong.

Trial runs

Professional decorators make up mood boards for clients showing swatches of paints, papers and fabrics, and you can do something similar using this journal (see page 30). The key to using a mood board is understanding both light and scale. The shade you love in a tiny swatch might be oppressive or sickly once it is covering all four walls of your dining room. The vibrant tartan you so admire might have a startling effect once you see it used to cover a large piece of furniture.

That is why it is always worth buying a roll of wallpaper, a good-sized fabric swatch or a sample pot of paint before making your final decision. Try living with them – move the samples around the room and see how they look at different times of day and night.

Choosing a scheme

Forget about what colours are supposedly in or out of fashion. Instead, look around your own home and gather together some of the things you love. Over the years we all build up our own colour palette that we feel comfortable with and enjoy. It makes sense to use this as a basis for decorating our homes. That is not to say you should not be open to other possibilities – easy-to-use base colours can be layered with more dynamic shades.

Do not worry about what goes with what. In truth, you can mix any colour with any other; what matters is their intensity. Colour fashions come and go, which is why I have evolved ranges over the years that are guaranteed to complement each other whether they were launched last year or ten years ago.

Tip
Avoid getting locked into a colour scheme.

TOP, ABOVE AND OPPOSITE: *Colour and pattern are used in a contemporary way in this dining room. The steel grey of the taffeta curtains and silver mica wallpaper are accented with splashes of red in the curtains' contrast lining and in the flower heads and fruit.*

Think of bright colours as the equivalent of spice when cooking: you do not want them to dominate, but simply to add a tang of unexpected flavour.

There are other ways of reflecting design trends in a room without overdosing on colour. Also, avoid any colour scheme that prevents anything else ever being brought into the room; always give yourself an escape route.

Low-key colour

You will achieve a better effect if your walls, sofas, floors and curtains don't all shout at each other. What you put on the walls and floors, the largest surfaces in a room, will determine the overall style. Keep contrasting colours for smaller chairs and accents such as pillows and flowers. I sometimes paint skirting boards (baseboards) in a darker shade, such as a brownish-black, to create a dramatic contrast.

Often I advise clients to keep walls and curtain fabric relatively plain – that way they know that they are guaranteed many years of use from them. Curtain trims, upholstery fabrics, rugs, pillows and lampshades are a much more flexible way of introducing bold colour into a room. And when your furniture is stunning, you do not necessarily want to add a lot of pattern and colour as well.

I do not often use white, but when combined with black for definition it can give a dramatic and graphic look that is clean, sharp and modern.

OPPOSITE AND ABOVE RIGHT: *Use neutrals to prevent stronger colours overwhelming. Neutrals predominate in the restful palette of the living room opposite. In the bedroom above right, neutral curtains and carpet offset bold tartan walls. In both rooms, red is an accent.*

Because brilliant white can soon look dead and grey, choose an off-white shade instead. There is sometimes a temptation to paint a modern house or apartment all white or off-white, but I prefer to use a simple, controlled, harmonious, two- or three-colour palette. Let your possessions, such as your art, collections and furniture, provide the detail and richness.

Deep colour

Painting a room a deep colour takes courage, but it can be effective. It is a particularly good way of making small rooms look special and also a means of smoothing out odd-shaped rooms. Rooms that have deep-toned or dark-coloured walls benefit from lots of pictures and ornaments to break up the solid colour.

Introducing pattern

Texture can, of course, take the place of pattern, creating a relaxed, modern look, but a room without any pattern may look bland. Try to introduce pattern so as to give a room direction without swamping it. There is no rule book that says you cannot mix florals with stripes, or plaids with paisleys – in fact, they can look wonderful together. The key is to avoid having equal amounts of each, which would create an unpleasant tension, and to be careful to have a little space between them.

Small-scale designs, such as spriggy flowers, work differently from larger ones. If you have a pelmet or a chair back in a big swirling pattern, it may be difficult not to cut the pattern off in its prime or slice a major motif in half. Smaller patterns avoid this problem and so can be used on almost anything. However, they look most fresh and modern when partnered with fairly calm accessories, such as cream lampshades, and accented in their deepest colour. For finishing touches on small-scale patterns, go for simplicity.

You have a choice – either cover everything in the room with the design or just use it on a few selected elements such as the walls. If you want to use an opulent fabric or wallpaper in a small room, prevent it from looking cluttered or fussy by limiting yourself to just that one pattern. If a room has only a small amount of wall space, then it can take a strong design.

Pattern brings vigour and excitement into a scheme, so do not be frightened of introducing it. But if you are cautious, then opt for a set of pillow covers to begin with, rather than reupholstering everything. And remember that solid colours do not date as fast as patterns.

Metallic and matt finishes

Reflective surfaces are important in interior design – the combination of mirror and candlelight, for example, never fails to delight. Over the last few years, it has been wonderful to see wallpaper and fabrics embrace the glamour of metallic finishes, creating an unashamedly luxurious look. When combined with well thought-out lighting, the effect is glorious.

However, if you are to achieve a sophisticated look rather than a tawdry one, it is important not to go too far. The role of solid colours has always been to provide a neutral foil for the more spectacular ingredients of a scheme. Contrasts are important, so remember that for every glossy surface you introduce, there should also be a matt one to enhance its impact.

ABOVE AND OPPOSITE: *I kept pattern to a minimum in this room in order not to detract from the wonderful Old Master paintings, which I set off with charcoal grey linen on the walls. However, there is very subtle pattern in the cream and taupe carpet, the blue stamped-velvet upholstery of the dining chairs, and the eye-catching blue braid edging of the dress curtains.*

Interior design from start to finish

The rest of this journal is divided into room-by-room chapters, with pages for you to fill in at the end of each chapter. You can obviously use just the pages that are appropriate to your own requirements, but they are designed to help you throughout the whole interior design process. Below is a list of the pages you can fill in that are in each chapter.

* **Floor plan:** your own drawing, which will help you plan the lighting and furniture arrangement

* **Questionnaire:** the initial questions to ask yourself to pinpoint what you need to do

* **Job analysis:** a breakdown of the work to be done and the materials and colours of all elements of the job

* **Work timetable:** a quick-reference record and overview of what has to happen when

* **Sourcing records:** details of the ordering of all items for window treatments, flooring, lighting, wallcovering and paints, furniture, upholstery and accessories

Home questionnaire

Ask yourself the following questions about your home in general, and write the answers below. (Use pencil so you can update it or change your mind.) Once you have narrowed down what needs to be done, fill in the questionnaires for the relevant rooms (see pages 42, 64, 90, 104, 132 and 134).

1 Do you feel that the space in your home is adequate?

_____

_____

2 If not, for what aspects do you need more space?

_____

_____

3 Could these be created from existing space or would you need to extend the house?

_____

_____

4 Do you need to install any security systems or music systems? Would the decoration be affected and, if so, in which rooms?

_____

_____

_____

5 Which, if any, of the existing facilities need to be improved?

_____

_____

_____

6 Which jobs are most urgent?

_____

_____

7 Would it be more efficient in terms of budget and schedule to do some jobs together, and, if so, which?

_____

_____

_____

_____

Mood boards

A mood board is an extension of the job analysis you compile for each room (see pages 44, 66, 92, 106, 136 and 138), allowing you to visualize how all the elements of a scheme will interrelate. Not only is it a good reference source, but it also will help you spot things that don't work before you have committed to them. Here is how to make one:

1 You will need a good-sized piece of cardboard – about 450 x 600mm (18 x 24in), or size A2 – for each room.

2 Gather together paint, wallpaper and fabric swatches of the major elements of the room: ceiling, cornice (cove), walls, woodwork, window treatments, upholstery, pillows or other fabrics. If possible use pinking shears to cut them out, and ideally cut them to sizes roughly in proportion to the area they will cover in the room. For tiles, flooring or anything else you don't have swatches for, use a paint swatch in that colour. Keep swatches you do not use in the pockets of each divider in this journal.

3 With glue or double-sided tape, stick the swatches to the cardboard, positioning them if possible in approximately the same position in which they will be used in the room (ceiling paint at the top, flooring at the bottom, walls in between).

4 Add photos where available of furniture, accessories, lighting, Venetian blinds, radiator covers, etc, plus any inspirational pictures that capture the look you want to achieve. Label everything clearly.

Briefing checklist

It is safest not to assume anything when briefing suppliers; try to discuss all aspects, anticipate every eventuality and spell everything out, preferably in writing.

Your contract should include:
* completion date
* cost based on a firm quotation rather than just an estimate
* amount and date payable for any deposit
* date by which further payment instalments and balance are to be paid
* defects liability period (eg, three months), during which any defects that arise from faulty workmanship or materials supplied by the supplier will be put right by them at no extra cost
* agreed percentage of payment to withhold till end of defects liability period.

Here is a checklist of important points to discuss:

Painting
* All painted surfaces: decorator to wash down, fill and sand if necessary, and prepare with undercoat and two topcoats (or three if necessary). Application of lining paper prior to painting to be discussed.
* All new woodwork: decorator to treat with knotting compound, fill, sand and prime beforehand.
* Colours/special finishes to be approved by self before application.
* Type of paint to be agreed (eg, anti-fungal paint for bathrooms and kitchen, heat-resistant paint for radiators).

Wallpapering
* All walls to be stripped of existing paper, washed, filled, sanded and sized.
* Cross-lining to be discussed.

Tiling
* Old tiles to be removed and wall filled/replastered.
* Breakage allowance and number of special tiles such as corner tiles and edge tiles.

Flooring
* Removal of existing flooring; application of damp-proof membrane, screed, insulation or plywood; type of adhesive (and grouting for floor tiles) and type of sealant are all issues to clarify.

Floor plans

Pages of graph paper in each chapter can be used for your own floor plans. You can prepare simple sketches or neat, finished plans, whichever you prefer. Samples of both are shown here, along with examples of symbols you can use.

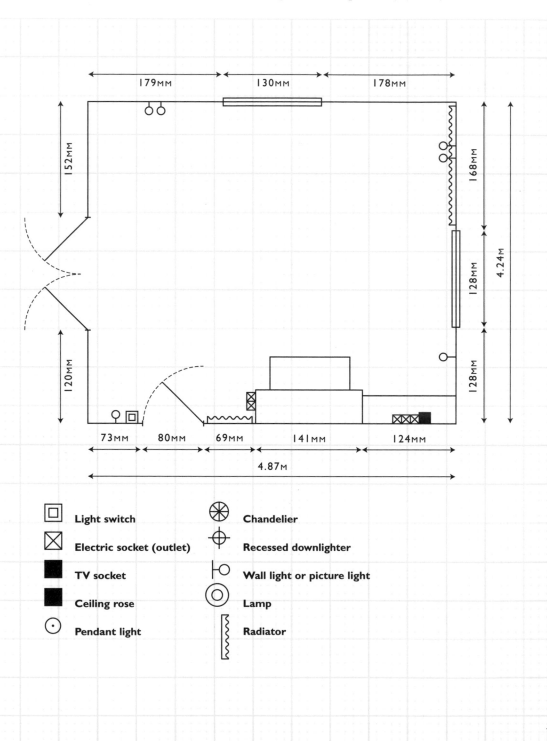

⊡	Light switch	⊕ Chandelier
⊠	Electric socket (outlet)	Recessed downlighter
■	TV socket	Wall light or picture light
■	Ceiling rose	Lamp
⊙	Pendant light	Radiator

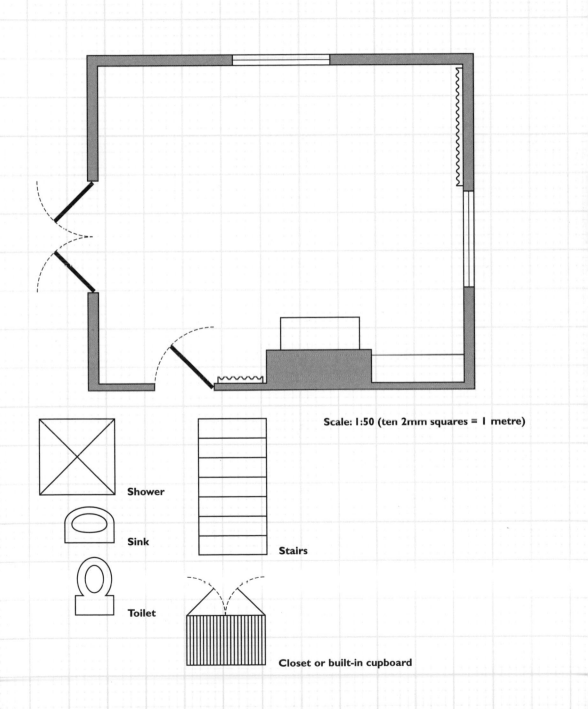

Scale: 1:50 (ten 2mm squares = 1 metre)

Shower

Sink

Toilet

Stairs

Closet or built-in cupboard

Making an impact

The most important fact to keep in mind when decorating an entry hall is that it is a room in its own right. People think of it as a through-route to other more important rooms, and so they rarely spend as much time, energy or money on the decoration. The flip side of the coin is that because no one spends much time in the entry hall, you can be daring with the decor.

ABOVE: *In this newly built apartment, the spacious entry hall seems to flow into the adjacent living area through the tall double doors. The mellow palette and the glow from the dramatic lantern add to the inviting atmosphere.*

What to showcase... and what not to

If you are lucky enough to have a large entry hall, it can be the ideal place in which to display treasured possessions, be they paintings, oriental rugs, fine pieces of furniture or one grand *pièce de résistance*. In other words, an entry hall offers the opportunity to create your own private gallery. It is also the perfect setting in which to create pockets of interest and excitement: a chance to whet the visual appetite of guests.

It helps enormously if you can resist the temptation to use the entry hall as a dumping ground for various pieces of household flotsam, such as coats, shoes, dog leashes, umbrellas, bicycles or buggies. If you do not have a large closet or cupboard where such essential but unattractive items can be stored, then you should think seriously about having one built. The entry hall should be a calming, uncluttered space – somewhere you can mentally catch your breath on entering the house.

Making a good impression

Good lighting is also important – it should not be so bright that it makes visitors blink after coming in from the darkness outside, nor should it be so dim that they run the risk of tripping on the rug. It should have a warm and welcoming feel in the winter and in the evening, and a calm atmosphere in the summer and in daylight.

Once you have achieved the perfect canvas on which to work, introduce much-loved furnishings and decorative items that convey the message you want to send about your house.

Although entry halls are primarily rooms in which we spend little time, they can be enjoyable places to sit, so if you have enough space, include a sofa or chairs. And even if the room is modest in size, you may be able to achieve a similar effect with a small, comfortable chair.

It's usually a good idea to carry the wall treatment of the hallway up the stairway in order to avoid any awkward breaks, as the two areas are usually viewed together. For the same reason, the decorative treatment of the landing needs to relate to that of the stairway.

ABOVE: *The rich amethyst paint colour in this stairway is warm and welcoming, and is echoed in the entry hall downstairs. The bookcases lined with books provide their own abstract pattern.*

Improving proportions

Don't despair if your own entry hall is flawed in some way – too small, too narrow, too low, too dark. It is usually possible to camouflage imperfections through clever decorating, and sometimes even to make features of them. Think about whether you could take a creative view and make good any faults in your own entry hall with panache.

Clever distractions

The size and shape of windows can be altered visually through curtain treatments. If a window is, say, too narrow, hang a curtain pole that is much wider than the window so that you can give the illusion of width through the curtains being more to the side. If the window has an awkward

ABOVE AND RIGHT: *In this dramatic entry hall, a jade Buddha hovers on a Perspex (Plexiglas) shelf above a Regency cabinet flanked by Klismos chairs (above), and a pierced concrete jalousie screen veiled with sheer linen lets in light and air (right).*

Tip

Distract attention from what is unattractive by highlighting the beauty of something else.

shape – a triangular top perhaps – then use blinds to conceal the unsightly design.

An entry hall that has too low a ceiling can be given a sense of scale by making doors larger and hanging curtains from cornice to floor. An entry hall that is dark and narrow can be enormously improved through the clever positioning of lighting and mirrors. A long, thin

entry hall can be made to look less like a corridor by painting the side walls in a lighter colour and the end walls in a warmer, deeper or stronger tone; hanging a striking picture on one of the end walls and lighting it dramatically will also help.

Creating continuity

Although the entry hall must be considered as an independent area, doors leading off from it give tantalizing glimpses into other rooms. It is therefore important to think about the views you create – not only of the adjacent rooms, but also of the entry hall from these rooms. This is particularly true if the doors are often kept open, because you do not want a jarring effect as the eye is led from one space into another.

On the surface

You may be tempted to choose a bolder than usual colour for your entry hall, and certainly this can create an immediate impact. But you do have to consider how it will blend with the rooms around it. Keeping colours and wall decorations similar but changing the flooring is a good way of linking one room to the next while at the same time emphasizing where one room stops and another begins. Hard floors – usually wood or

ABOVE, TOP RIGHT AND ABOVE RIGHT: *In this narrow, windowless entry hall, red lacquer walls echo the drawing room carpet, while gilt urns, a cut-glass vase, a gilt and marble console table and a Venetian mirror add sparkle*

stone – are ideal in entry halls, as they can withstand a lot of wear and tear, whereas carpet may be the preferred choice for adjacent rooms. Rugs are useful in areas like this, too, as they can be replaced more easily than wall-to-wall carpet.

Stairways In many entry halls, the stairs are the major feature. Safety is important here, so avoid using any floor covering with a slippery surface, and make sure that it is securely fixed in place. Carpet runners held in place by brass or steel rods and showing off the wood at the edges give a more classic look than fitted stair carpet taken to the edges.

Adding interest

The walls of stairways can be a good place to hang a collection of pictures that you particularly enjoy looking at. They will give you pleasure every time you use the stairs.

If there is space on a half-landing, where the stairs change direction (or on the landing, in fact), consider squeezing in a pair of chairs,

ABOVE: *On the stairwell of my own house the watercolours and drawings are all linked through my personal associations with them.*

a window seat, an armoire or some built-in bookcases, any of which will serve a practical purpose as well as 'furnishing' this area, making it almost a room in its own right.

Stairways are a great place to hang pictures that mean something to you.

Floor Plan: **Entry Hall and Stairway**

Questionnaire: **Entry hall and stairway**

Ask yourself the following questions about your entry hall and stairway, if any, and write the answers below. (Use a pencil so you can update it or change your mind.)

1   How suitable is it as an entry hall, and is the space adequate for your needs?

2   Are any structural alterations needed?

3   Could the lighting be improved and, if so, how?

4   Are there enough electrical sockets (outlets) in the right places?

5   Does the architectural style detract from or add to the overall ambience?

6   What are the views like, both from inside to outside and through internal doorways?

7   What are the entry hall's and staircase's best features and how could these be accentuated?

8   What are their faults and are there any possible solutions?

9   Would it make the entry hall more functional if radiators or air-conditioning units were moved?

10   Is there an existing feature that would make an eye-catching focal point? If so, how could it be dressed up to look really special?

11   Would the entry hall benefit from having more than one focal point?

12 Do you have an idea for some other focal point you would like to introduce?

13 Would it be possible to fit in some more storage?

14 Are the entry hall and stairway in need of redecoration?

15 Are there any colours/woods you cannot change that will affect your scheme?

16 Will you need to replace the window treatments?

17 Do the flooring/carpet/rugs need to be replaced? Do you want to consider a different treatment?

18 Which furniture can you continue to use as it is, and what new furniture will you need?

19 If money were no object, how would you alter the entry hall and stairs?

20 Would it be possible to do any of your 'dream' changes from the previous question?

21 What are your priorities, and how are you going to allocate the budget you are working within?

22 If you do not have a hallway, would it be possible to create an entry area, either by screening off part of the living area or by adding an extension?

Job analysis: **Entry hall and stairway**

surface	work to be done	materials and colours	comments
	DECORATION		
Ceiling			
paint			
Cornice (cove)			
paint			
Walls			
paint			
paper			
fabric			
Woodwork			
paint			
	STRUCTURAL ALTERATIONS		
Radiators			
type			
paint			
covers			
Electrics			
Plumbing			
radiators, if necessary			

Work Timetable: **Entry hall and stairway**

job	supplier	start/completion dates	action required	job completed	comments
DECORATION					
Ceiling					
paint					
Cornice (cove)					
paint					
Walls					
paint					
paper					
fabric					
Woodwork					
paint					
STRUCTURAL ALTERATIONS					
Radiators					
type					
paint					
covers					
Electrics					
Plumbing					
radiators, if necessary					

Sourcing record: **Entry hall and stairway**

Supplied by/manufacturer

___

Number of windows

___

Description: style, heading, length, material(s)

___

Main fabric: reference number, colour, width, pattern repeat

___

Main fabric: price per metre/yard, amount required, estimated cost

___

Edgings/trimmings (if any): description, reference number, colour, estimated cost

___

Lining (if any): description, reference number, colour, estimated cost

___

Interlining (if any): type, estimated cost

___

Tiebacks (if any): description, reference number, colour, estimated cost

___

Poles/rods, holdbacks, etc: description, reference number, colour, estimated cost

___

Estimated making and hanging cost

___

Total estimated cost

___

Comments

___

Sourcing record: **Entry hall and stairway**

Supplied by/manufacturer

Description: material, suitability (light/normal/heavy domestic)

Reference number, colour, width

Price per square/linear metre/yard, amount required, estimated cost

---

Fitting/laying estimated cost, total estimated cost

Comments

Sourcing record: **Entry hall and stairway**

LIGHTING

Supplied by/manufacturer

Descriptions, reference numbers, colours

Price per light, number of lights, estimated cost

Installation estimated cost

Total estimated cost

Comments

Sourcing record: **Entry hall and stairway**

WALLCOVERING AND PAINTS

Supplied by/manufacturer

Descriptions, reference numbers, colours

Wallcovering price per roll, amount required, estimated cost

Paint estimated cost

Labour estimated cost, total estimated cost

Comments

Sourcing record: **Entry hall and stairway**

FURNITURE

Supplied by/manufacturer

Descriptions

Reference numbers, colours, sizes

Price per item

Total estimated cost

Comments

Sourcing record: **Entry hall and stairway**

Supplied by/manufacturer

_____

Descriptions: fabrics and trimmings

_____

Reference numbers, colours, widths

_____

Price per metre/yard, amount required, fabric estimated cost

_____

Labour estimated cost, total estimated cost

_____

Comments

_____

Sourcing record: **Entry hall and stairway**

ACCESSORIES

Supplied by/manufacturer

_____

Descriptions

_____

Reference numbers, colours

_____

Price per item

_____

Total estimated cost

_____

Comments

_____

The big picture

Living rooms are for living in. The days of the stiff, gracious – and barely used – formal drawing room are limited. Now that the barriers are down and rooms are spaces – spaces to entertain, relax, maybe work, or eat – it is important to zone your activities, and to do this effectively you need to analyse the functions of the room.

Planning the space

Imagine how the room will work when it is being used by the family or for entertaining guests, and think about when they are most likely to be in here. You might have a living room that is used far more in the summer than the winter, for instance, or in the evening much more than in the daytime. If this is a space you plan to use mainly by day, it is important to study the natural light and consider ways of boosting it if necessary.

Plan the space first and make architectural changes if necessary before making any major decorating decisions. On page 64, write down what you intend to do in the room, whether it is watching television, reading, playing games or chatting to friends. Never skimp on this stage. Take measurements and try out your plans with a scale drawing (see pages 32–3 and 63).

You must also assess the strengths and weaknesses of the room in terms of proportion, architecture and permanent features (see pages 13–15). I don't like seeing blocked-in fireplaces or chimney breasts without a function, so even if you can't use the fireplace, I think it's nice to have one there.

In my own fireplace (see page 52) in my living area, there is a problem with the size of the flue, so there was no way I could have a functioning fireplace. Instead I installed a basket of rock-crystal logs, which when lit from above look just magical.

ABOVE: *This is a room used for reading, playing games and spending time with family and friends, so the seating is arranged around the fireplace and there are plenty of reading lamps. The walls, bookcases, panelling and fireplace are all painted in the same rich toffee shade, a trick that makes a busy room feel very calm.*

Building the look

Once flaws have been masked, you can bring in layers of decoration to achieve a really glorious effect. Find an item you love and use it to hold the rest of the scheme together. Take inspiration from its shape, colour and texture and make these the basis for decorating decisions. It is much easier to work this way around than to decorate a room and then begin the search for the perfect focal point.

Tip
When buying a rug, look out for one that doesn't have a central motif, as it will be less restrictive when you are arranging furniture.

A beautiful patterned rug, elegant wallpaper or magnificent curtain fabric might be the starting point. Don't despair if you can't afford all three: buy well for one and it will make a world of difference. Then raid the rest of your home for the finest pieces of furniture or the best paintings or other pieces of art you have.

Neutral schemes

Always err on the side of simplicity. There is much to be said for using neutrals as a basis for a scheme, because it then allows you to bring colour in through the upholstery fabrics, pillows, rugs, lamps, pictures or flowers. These are far more versatile than wallpaper or carpet.

Living rooms in particular lend themselves to neutrals, but they should be 'happy' neutrals – not cold colours, which have a depressing effect. Neutral living rooms also contrast well with dining rooms, which are a more obvious place in which to use strong colours. Introducing themes and colours onto a neutral canvas has another

TOP AND ABOVE: *In my living area (top) I wanted a light-filled, shimmering space. The rug was my starting point f or the scheme. In my son's small living room (above) the wallcovering, sofa and carpet were all kept neutral, with colour added in the rug and accessories.*

advantage: it makes it much easier to subtly alter a room from winter to summer or from day to evening, ringing the changes according to your mood. This approach makes accessorizing even more important.

Focal points

Each room needs a centrepiece of some description, to set the tone for the rest of the scheme and tie the look together. It is also useful because it will draw the eye away from less pleasing aspects of the room. Often the focal point is already in the room – a handsome fireplace, for example, naturally draws the eye towards it. Enhance it with fire irons, a fender seat and a wonderful painting over the mantelpiece and you immediately create an anchor around which to position the seating.

Creating new focal points

To create a focal point in a room that has none, the golden rule is to think big. In a small space, one big object brings a resonance that will immediately make you think the room must be larger than it is. In a big one, it is even more

ABOVE: *We based the scheme of this room around the large Renaissance painting, which dominates the room. In order to hang the painting in pole position, we took the fireplace out and, inverting tradition, built out the bookcases on either side. The Aubusson carpet is in the same palette of reds, creams and golds.*

important to have something that can live up to the generous proportions. It might be an over-scaled piece of furniture, such as a bookcase or armoire, or an enormous painting or mirror.

Positioning other pieces around the centrepiece in such a way that nothing detracts from its overall effect will also ensure it becomes a focal point – but be sure to give it space, so the eye will rest on it as you enter the room. Depending on what it is, consider whether your anchor piece needs 'dressing' in any way; should it be specially lit perhaps or be placed against a different background colour?

Tip
Create a theatrical look by displaying a collection of plates, hats or some other three-dimensional items on one wall.

ABOVE: *In the high-ceilinged living room of my former apartment, the divided mirror balances the window treatment as well as providing a focal point and adding to the natural light and sense of space. I took the rug and bergère chairs with me to my new house (see page 52).*

Focal points are not only about having a big, important piece. It is also fun to have smaller tableaux that you enjoy once you are sitting down and relaxing. A collection of small objects, for example, can draw attention when displayed well at sitting height, like the tablescape on page 53.

Seating areas

Seating areas Because living areas fulfil many uses, it is important that they are laid out with some flexibility. It is a depressing sight to walk into a room where the sofa and chairs are arranged in a U-shape around the television. Ideally, put the TV somewhere else in the house altogether, but if this is not possible, at least try not to draw such obvious attention to it.

Groupings

Although houses should be designed primarily with the owners in mind, you should also allow for entertaining. It makes no sense to have a dining area that seats twelve people if you can seat only six in the living area, so have extra seating available, such as a fender seat, a window seat or an ottoman that doubles as a coffee table. (Choosing a colour for the dining chairs that also goes with your living area scheme will mean you can use them there when entertaining.)

You might plan to have two sitting areas in a room: a more intimate one around the fire for family or a small group of friends; and a separate

ABOVE: *This large living room has two seating areas – the other is pictured on page 61. The sofa, two green silk velvet bergère chairs and two stools (in the same fabric as the curtains) are arranged around a beaten-brass coffee table with a glass-covered silverleaf top.*

one – perhaps near a window and arranged round a table – that can be used for playing games, studying or reading. This way, when you find yourself with more guests than usual, you can seat everyone comfortably just by moving some of the key pieces around. A very large living area demands several seating areas, so plan these before buying furniture or dragging heavy pieces around.

ABOVE: *In this room I set a two-seater and a three-seater sofa at right angles and placed a huge glass coffee table in the centre of the room. A round glass-topped table sits between the sofas, and deep but narrow glass side tables at the other ends of the sofas.*

The celebrated interior designer Elsie de Wolfe advised that you should never have one chair stuck out on a limb, as invariably someone rather shy will sit on it and then feel too embarrassed to move closer to everyone else.

A range of seating

A really cosy armchair in which you can lie back with your feet on a stool is not a luxury but an essential. However, any living area benefits from having a range of seating in different styles and shapes: a sofa on which to sprawl and at least a couple of chairs that can be pulled into position

at will. Anyone who has suffered backache will know that deep, squashy sofas are not always the kindest. People prefer softer or harder, lower or

OPPOSITE BELOW, ABOVE AND RIGHT: *Here, a pair of sofas face each other either side of the fireplace. The brocade upholstery and braid trim on the Louis XV bergère chair arms echo the colour scheme, while a gaufrage leather fender seat also picks up on the strong red.*

higher seating, according to their height, physical characteristics and personal preferences. At any rate, a chair for reading is not necessarily the chair you are most relaxed in when chatting, and a lightweight chair is easier to pull up to a grouping or draw aside for a private read.

Now sit down and look around. If you were to offer a guest a drink, would it be obvious where he or she could put it down? There is little point having enough chairs if you don't have surfaces within easy reaching distance of them. And if those surfaces mark easily, it is up to you to protect them in some way. The aim is to induce a feeling of well-being and relaxation.

> **Tip**
> It's good to have a wing chair in a room because it adds a height contrast.

Furnishing with fabric

A successful decorating scheme brings together many ingredients to form a cohesive whole. Fabrics lend softness, a sense of being cocooned, to a room. This subliminal message can be accentuated through the colours, patterns and types of fabric you choose. Silk, for example, remains popular not only for its luxurious look but also because it has such a tactile quality. The same is true of many other choices, such as chenille, velvet, linen, crewelwork and voile.

Principal fabrics

Grand curtain treatments work well when the windows are tall enough, and beautifully dressed windows will never go out of date because they are often the focal point of a room. It is not enough to choose a wonderful fabric: you must also put some thought into all the other aspects of a window treatment.

For upholstery and slipcovers, choose colours that harmonize rather than match each other. Find one fabric that you love, and choose all the other fabrics to go with it. You may decide to use it only on something small, but it's still your 'anchor'. A sofa is a good-sized piece of furniture, and many living areas have two or even more. Covering them in fabric that is at the opposite end of the colour spectrum from the walls – red

ABOVE LEFT, ABOVE AND OPPOSITE: *Making a splash with a strong colour strikes a contemporary note, while trimmings can echo other colours in a room's palette, as with the gold-on-velvet border, metallic cord and bobble fringing used here on a tablecloth, sofa and pillows.*

sofas in a green room, for example – will usually jar the eye, so choose a colour that harmonizes rather than contrasts with the walls, especially if your room is small.

All-important detail

Pillows are an indispensable part of any scheme. They not only are essential to comfort and make seating look more inviting, but they can be used to introduce contrasting colour, pattern and texture to a scheme. However, they should not

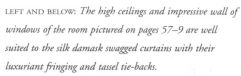

LEFT AND BELOW: *The high ceilings and impressive wall of windows of the room pictured on pages 57–9 are well suited to the silk damask swagged curtains with their luxuriant fringing and tassel tie-backs.*

LEFT: *The aqua and gold tones of the window treatment and carpet are picked up in the silk brocade of the charming little Louis XV gilded wood footstool finished with a narrow gold braid.*

be arranged so stiffly that guests feel too inhibited to rearrange them. As with everything else in the room, they should have both a visual and a practical use. Throws, often coupled with pillows, are a way of layering softness and drawing the eye away from slightly lived-in upholstery fabrics.

Trimmings are worth their weight in gold because they quite literally give a decorative scheme a professional edge, accentuating the lines of furniture, highlighting smart tailoring and defining window treatments and pillows. Piping, braids, fringing, bobbles and beads, rope and tassels all offer enormous scope. There is a wealth of colours, sizes and designs to choose from, or you can have them custom-made to match your fabric or pick up the colours in your decorative scheme.

Tip
Use trimmings to pull the colours in a room together.

The personal touch

Remember that you are your own client and you want a room that is unique to you, rather than a replica of someone else's home. Your signature should be apparent in every aspect of your house.

Adding character

Often it is the combination of old and new that gives a house character – a welcoming, timeless feeling of a heritage that has evolved and mellowed over generations. If you want to create this effect from scratch, don't get everything from one kind of shop. Use art and antiques to create pattern and texture, always choosing items that you genuinely like.

Instant updates

Do not write off your old possessions because you are seeking a new look. They may just need a little renovation to give them a whole new lease of life. Sometimes I encourage clients to walk around their homes removing treasures from one room in order to dress another. A fresh location can draw attention to something that has been neglected in the past few years.

ABOVE: *To display a rock crystal collection, we adapted the alcove shelving in this room using mirror, a custom architrave and LED lighting.*

Not all rooms require a complete overhaul. Many of them can be given a lift simply by editing some things out, repositioning others and introducing a few new buys that will inject life into a room. It is amazing how different a room can look with a new rug or pillows, a change of lampshades or better-hung pictures. Accessories and flowers also help just-decorated rooms become truly finished.

Hanging pictures

When you are updating a room, do not simply put the framed pictures back as they were before. Instead, rationalize and rehang them – this is worth doing every few years in any house, as things can easily get cluttered.

Tip
Old lampshades and faded pillows date a room more than anything. Changing them can provide an instant uplift.

Many people have paintings or prints on their walls but have paid little attention to displaying them really well. The golden rule is to group them wherever possible, particularly if they are small. You can really only do this by trial and error, relying on your instinct, but I find it helpful to start with a big central picture. Plan the entire arrangement on the floor first, keeping the space tight between the frames and aiming for a grouping that looks balanced. Good lighting is also crucial: if you want to enjoy a fine painting, it makes no sense to hang it in semi-darkness.

Displaying collections

Collections bring immediate interest and character into a room. They are expressive of your personality because often they are linked to your interests, the places you have travelled or something in your family's history.

Tip
Think about where you are going to position your pictures before you start decorating and furnishing a room.

Keep a collection of objects together; there is no point diluting their impact by separating them. Whereas a piece of coloured glass, say, may be unprepossessing, a group makes a bold visual statement. Think about where to position the collection so that it can be enjoyed to best advantage. Usually this means placing it at eye level – but bear in mind that this could mean eye level from sitting height. Make sure the accent lighting does justice to it.

Designing a room around a collection can be doubly rewarding: you will have created a beautiful space and a backdrop for something you love.

BELOW LEFT AND BELOW: *Two glittering displays. Rock crystals in mirrored alcoves (see page 61) are lit by LED lights inset into shelves with mirrored inlays, while a Victorian coffee service sits alongside modern saucerless cups on a 1930s tray.*

A collection provides inspiration for colour, pattern and texture.

Floor plan: **Living area**

Questionnaire: **Living area**

Ask yourself the following questions about your living area, and write the answers below. (Use a pencil so you can update it or change your mind.)

1 Who uses this room, and for what?

2 How suitable is it for these functions, and is the space adequate for your needs?

3 Are any structural alterations needed?

4 Could the lighting be improved and, if so, how?

5 Are there enough electrical sockets (outlets) in the right places?

6 Does the architectural style detract from or add to the overall ambience?

7 What are the views like, both from inside to outside and through internal doorways?

8 What are the room's best features and how could these be accentuated?

9 What are its faults and are there any possible solutions?

10 Would it make the room more functional if radiators or air-conditioning units were moved?

11 Is there an existing feature that would make an eye-catching focal point? If so, how could it be dressed up to look really special?

12 Would the room benefit from having more than one focal point?

13 Do you have an idea for some other focal point you would like to introduce?

14 Would it be possible to fit in some more storage?

15 Is the room in need of redecoration?

16 Are there any colours/woods you cannot change (such as a marble fireplace or a mahogany mantelpiece) that will affect your scheme?

17 Will you need to replace the window treatments?

18 Do the flooring/carpet/rugs need to be replaced? Do you want to consider a different treatment?

19 Which furniture can you continue to use as it is, which can you use if you reupholster it, and what new furniture will you need?

20 If money were no object, how would you alter this room?

21 Would it be possible to do any of the 'dream' changes from the previous question?

22 What are your priorities, and how are you going to allocate the budget you are working within?

Job analysis: Living area

surface	work to be done	materials and colours	comments
	DECORATION		
Ceiling			
paint			
Cornice (cove)			
paint			
Walls			
paint			
paper			
fabric			
Woodwork			
paint			
	STRUCTURAL ALTERATIONS		
Radiators			
type			
paint			
covers			
Electrics			
Plumbing			
radiators, if necessary			

Work Timetable: Living area

job	supplier	start/completion dates	action required	job completed	comments
DECORATION					
Ceiling					
paint					
Cornice (cove)					
paint					
Walls					
paint					
paper					
fabric					
Woodwork					
paint					
STRUCTURAL ALTERATIONS					
Radiators					
type					
paint					
covers					
Electrics					
Plumbing					
radiators, if necessary					

Sourcing record: **Living area**

Supplied by/manufacturer

_____

Number of windows

_____

Description: style, heading, length, material(s)

_____

Main fabric: reference number, colour, width, pattern repeat

_____

Main fabric: price per metre/yard, amount required, estimated cost

_____

Edgings/trimmings (if any): description, reference number, colour, estimated cost

_____

Lining (if any): description, reference number, colour, estimated cost

_____

Interlining (if any): type, estimated cost

_____

Tiebacks (if any): description, reference number, colour, estimated cost

_____

Poles/rods, holdbacks, etc: description, reference number, colour, estimated cost

_____

Estimated making and hanging cost

_____

Total estimated cost

_____

Comments

_____

Sourcing record: **Living area**

FLOORING

Supplied by/manufacturer

Description: material, suitability (light/normal/heavy domestic)

Reference number, colour, width

Price per square/linear metre/yard, amount required, estimated cost

Fitting/laying estimated cost, total estimated cost

Comments

Sourcing record: **Living area**

LIGHTING

Supplied by/manufacturer

Descriptions, reference numbers, colours

Price per light, number of lights, estimated cost

Installation estimated cost

Total estimated cost

Comments

Sourcing record: **Living area**

Supplied by/manufacturer

Descriptions, reference numbers, colours

Wallcovering price per roll, amount required, estimated cost

Paint estimated cost

Labour estimated cost, total estimated cost

Comments

Sourcing record: **Living area**

FURNITURE

Supplied by/manufacturer

Descriptions

Reference numbers, colours, sizes

Price per item

Total estimated cost

Comments

Sourcing record: **Living area**

UPHOLSTERY

Supplied by/manufacturer

Descriptions: fabrics and trimmings

Reference numbers, colours, widths

Price per metre/yard, amount required, fabric estimated cost

Labour estimated cost, total estimated cost

Comments

Sourcing record: **Living area**

ACCESSORIES

Supplied by/manufacturer

Descriptions

Reference numbers, colours

Price per item

Total estimated cost

Comments

Creating a mood

You may use your dining area for formal lunches, probably at weekends, but it is more likely a predominantly nocturnal space – and lighting, colours and textures have to be chosen with this in mind. You also need to think about how the dining room links to adjacent rooms, or the dining area in an open-plan living area to other spaces.

Maintaining an illusion

By day you may want to screen it off, but when entertaining friends at night it is wonderful to allow tantalizing glimpses of a beautifully laid table and shimmering candles. Even the most jaded of your guests will be encouraged to rise to the occasion if the dining area – and therefore the food and wine – looks inviting. The scene is now set for a memorable and stimulating evening.

It is essential in a dining area to maintain an illusion of perfection. If it is a separate room that you use rarely, this fact should not be apparent. Or if the dining area has to do double duty as a work area, that too should not be obvious. Tarnished silver, dusty surfaces or untidy corners where children's homework has been thrown aside will detract from the magic.

TOP AND ABOVE: *A table setting can transform a dining room. Here, Brussels lace and Derby plates create a delightful, Bacchanalian mood, and place names in delicate silver holders ensure that guests feel welcome.*

There are practical aspects to consider at the beginning. To establish how well your dining room works from both a functional and an aesthetic point of view, answer the questions on pages 90–1. Once these issues have been considered and dealt with, you can concentrate on the decorative elements.

ABOVE: *After you have dealt with the basics of the interior design, you can indulge yourself with delightful tasks such as choosing and arranging centrepieces for the table. This silver stand, with its romantic, pastoral theme, makes a splendid container for flowers or fruit.*

Versatile dining rooms

If your home doesn't have room for a dedicated dining room, rather than sacrificing it entirely you might be able to find ways of utilizing the space better so that you get more than one use from the room. If you have a reasonable-sized entry hall, for example, the dining table could serve as a hall table by day, with the dining chairs against the walls out of the way (or in use in the living area). One of my previous dining rooms was also a billiards room. In another, the dining room doubled as a library (see page 76), providing not only an ideal floor-to-ceiling space in which to store an ever-increasing number of books but also an effective way of adding colour and cosiness.

Dining room storage

One thing I am passionate about is storage. Without it any room will look a mess, no matter how beautifully decorated it might be, and it's all the more vital in a dual-function room. In my previous dining room cum library, I lined one wall with deep floor-to-ceiling cupboards that

ABOVE: *I originally commissioned this cabinet with mirrored panels for the dining room in my apartment, pictured here, and liked it so much that I had it adapted for my present dining room (see page 84). It reflects light into the room, looks modern and yet is not overbearing. The base pictured here covers a long radiator and the top serves as a china cabinet.*

were concealed by hand-painted panels. The panels blended into the book-lined walls, so that at first glance they seemed to be purely a decorative addition, but behind them were all the essentials of elegant dining. In my present dining room (see page 84) I have a huge purpose-built cabinet with mirrored panels. It not only provides capacious storage but its flattering reflections make the most of candlelight.

BELOW AND RIGHT: *In my dining room that doubled as a library, the decorative panels concealed cupboards for plates, glasses and serving dishes, while the books were a talking point at dinner – as were the bay leaf place names.*

A dining room can be an ideal place to line walls with books.

Dedicated dining rooms

If you are lucky enough to have a separate dining room, you will know the joy of having a room that is set aside for entertaining, whether it is Sunday lunch for the family or a dinner party for friends. Eating, talking and laughing with people cements friendships and is integral to our well-being as social creatures.

Sense and sensibility

A dedicated dining room makes sense from a practical point of view. Dining areas in other rooms tend to become submerged in everyday clutter, so there is a great deal of tidying up to do before the cooking even begins. The whole process of entertaining runs so much more smoothly when there is a separate room in which

ABOVE AND RIGHT: *This spacious dining room is ideal for large-scale entertaining, with the mahogany dining table seating up to fourteen people. Plain white linen tablemats embroidered with drawn-thread work define each place setting. A silver bowl holding the low centrepiece adds to the classic look.*

all the paraphernalia of dining is kept, from
dinner services, wine glasses and table linen to
candelabras and soup tureens.

Having a room set aside to dine in means
that you can push the boundaries out a little
when decorating. After all, this is a room in
which you want to create visual impact and which

ABOVE: *A red velvet tablecloth, gold chargers, red glass
plates and red linen napkins make a dramatic background.
The glass cake stand holds antique mercury balls.*

is seen mostly at night. Put these factors together
and you realize you can be braver than usual – a
dining room needs some drama and sparkle, and

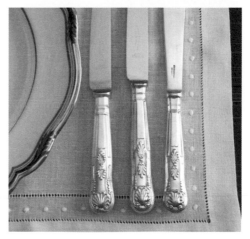

ABOVE, ABOVE RIGHT AND RIGHT: *Crystal, silver and china look wonderful in a dedicated dining room. Cut-crystal glasses provide a light show in their own right, and classic shell-pattern silverware always looks good. The china has a delicate rim of gold and blue.*

you can use colour much more intensely. Dining areas in other rooms have to conform to what is already in place, but separate dining rooms can have a different atmosphere. Their role is to create a small jolt of delight when guests walk in for the first time.

Dining room lighting

Lighting is probably the most important aspect of decorating a dining room. It should be subtle yet sparkling. There is nothing to beat candlelight in a dining room because it is flattering – to you, your guests and the room itself. However, you also need another source of low-level lighting so that guests can see what is on their plates and where to find the mustard pot. If you are carving or dishing up food from a serving table or sideboard, this needs to be well lit so that you can see what you are doing and there are no mishaps with a knife.

Tip
If you opt for a chandelier, go for something big and opulent – a small one will look half-hearted.

Wall lights, table lamps and picture lights are all good options, but bright overhead lights, other than chandeliers, are inappropriate at dinner. If it's too light, the atmosphere will be spoiled and people will look drained. Even chandeliers may need to be switched off. Not every room is suited to a chandelier, of course, and a similar effect can be achieved with ornate candelabras.

Creature comforts

The room should have easily controlled heating. Walking into a cold dining room is not conducive to good cheer – but once it is full of people, the temperature will rise, and an over-warm room can be equally uncomfortable.

The dining table

The focal point of any dining room is, of course, the table. How well you dress the table makes the difference between a moderately pleasant meal and an unforgettably elegant one.

Fundamental choices

If your table is beautiful, then show it off – there is no need to cover it with a cloth unless you are anxious to protect it. If you like to vary the look, then you could use a cloth for lunch parties and leave it uncovered at night to enjoy the reflection of candlelight on the polished surface. If your dining table is not attractive, however, do not despair. Once it is covered with a beautiful damask or linen cloth, no one would know whether it is Georgian mahogany or MDF.

Consider carefully how many dining chairs to buy. You may entertain eight people on average but if the table is large enough, perhaps when extended, to seat twelve, it makes sense to have twelve chairs for those rare occasions you need them. If you want your guests to linger, the chairs must be comfortable. If they are not upholstered, then at least have thick seat cushions on them.

Dressing it up

One of the joys of entertaining is, of course, dressing the table. As any chef will admit, much of the success of a meal lies in its presentation.

BELOW LEFT, BELOW AND OPPOSITE: *Around the dining table in my previous apartment, the monogrammed linen slipcovers echo the blue and white of the antique glass.*

Sometimes I like to leave a beautiful table quite bare and enjoy the wood.

Choosing the backdrop for your tablescape is
like preparing a stage set.

Not that table decoration is a substitute for stimulating conversation – the people gathered around the table are the most important ingredients for a successful evening. However, if you take care to set the scene properly, they will play their part with ease and enjoyment.

Setting a table is now a million miles away from simply getting out the wedding china and arranging it according to formal rules (nice as it is to do that on occasion). Try to build up sets of china and glasses, and a good selection of table linen, so that you can vary your table settings a little. Do not be constrained by what is available under the label 'tablecloth'. You can use almost any fabric – velvet, silk, antique

Tip
Combine antique china or glass with cheaper pieces to allow you to mix and match with ease.

ABOVE: *In this dining room the red of the walls and shelving is picked up in the red-rimmed china, red embroidery on the linen placemats and red flowers. A lot of contrast could have looked too busy.*

linen, upholstery fabric, dress material or even sheets or bedcovers.

Although I love tablecloths, I also own an enormous range of tablemats, from delicate Brussels lace and hand-embroidered antique linen to brightly coloured organza that would not disgrace an Indian wedding.

Setting the scene

Start by matching your approach to the occasion. A summer lunch demands light, pretty colours and flowers, while guests at a winter dinner party

will respond warmly to rich reds, oranges and other hot colours.

The colour scheme in your room can be a starting point, but dressing a table is also an opportunity to give the room a slightly different look – by adding vibrant colours, for example, to a calm, neutral room, or by introducing a touch of formality to a casual dining area.

ABOVE: *Here the flowers on the table pick up the decorative scheme, the starting point for which was the blue sky of the magnificent Jacob van Ruisdael landscape. (The room is also pictured on page 27.)*

Formal table settings look fabulous, but bending the rules a little will make the effect less predictable and more interesting. You could, for example, begin collecting glasses of one particular colour, such as cranberry, but from many different sources. You could also mix antique with modern; with the colour to unify the look, it would still be a success visually. What is of primary importance is that everything you use is maintained to a high standard – there must be no smudges on glasses or smears on silver. Always allow enough time when entertaining to check each item carefully.

Dramatic centrepieces

Carry the colour theme you have chosen through to the flowers and candles. Flowers have a truly magical effect upon a room – it is not just that they bring in a patch of brilliant colour often combined with enchanting scent, but that they bring life into a space. Whether you favour formal arrangements over informal ones, country

ABOVE: *The long, narrow dining table in my present house (also pictured in my former apartment, on page 80) seats fourteen. The flowers and the glasses recall the colour theme of the open-plan living area.*

blooms over the hothouse variety or house plants over cut flowers is entirely a personal choice. The important thing is to display them with flair.

A simple arrangement of flowers and fruit is ideal for lunch parties, while a more contrived display gives a sense of occasion to a more formal evening meal. They should be either low or high, so that guests seated opposite each other can talk over or under them. Be careful how you position candles, too – setting fire to the table centrepiece is an over-dramatic way of starting conversation.

Not every centrepiece has to be floral. You could use any distinctive grouping, from artichokes or Easter eggs to antique mercury balls. Just pile them up on a cake stand or in an appropriate bowl and make that the starting point for an inspirational table.

Kitchen dining

The kitchen is the hub of the household, the place where food is both prepared and enjoyed. For many families, the kitchen table is more than a place to eat – it is where people gravitate to do homework, write letters, use their laptop computers, read the newspaper or make phone calls. Therefore, before making crucial decorating decisions regarding the kitchen, you must first decide how and when you are likely to use the eating area.

A cheerful breakfast setting

It might be that your priority is to create a really lovely breakfast setting, rather than an intimate evening one. If you have sunlight flooding in first thing in the morning, then you could accentuate this with light colours and soft fabrics and choose tableware that has a fresh, daytime feel, different from the tableware you use in the evening.

Informal supper parties

It makes sense to eat breakfast and lunch here, but do not overlook it as a setting for evening entertaining, too. Even if your kitchen table has

ABOVE: *In the kitchen of my earlier house, I was able to fit six people around the table for lunch or informal suppers. The fresh blue and green colour scheme was inspired by my collection of plates.*

space for only four to six, you can still enjoy intimate supper parties. And a kitchen with enough room for a huge table means you can have large, informal gatherings of family and friends, allowing you to chat to your guests while you prepare the food (and they help). This kind of occasion can be so casual, however, that it is best suited to entertaining close friends.

Make breakfast an occasion, too.

ABOVE AND RIGHT: *The long banquette in the dining area of this kitchen sits on top of much-needed storage drawers. The end tables flanking it are built-in wine fridges, and an attractive countertop-mounted screen helps separate this area from the sink. The green and white scheme is followed through in the table setting.*

The key to creating a dining space within the kitchen is to integrate it in terms of design and colours, but also to find ways of separating it from the rest of the room, such as with a rug and more atmospheric lighting. Another option is to use different colours – perhaps a stronger backdrop on the dining-area walls to contrast with the rest of the kitchen. Visual barriers such as a peninsular unit or a screen also help to separate the dining area from the sink area. It goes without saying that good ventilation for the cooking zone is essential.

Practicalities

Hard flooring is best in kitchens, because it is durable and easy to clean, and a rug in the dining area will not only set the area apart but also soften the look and acoustics. Fabrics used on

chairs, at windows and for table linen help to make the dining area less clinical, too.

Good lighting is particularly important in the kitchen. Work stations require good illumination to prevent accidents. In addition, the eating-area lights need to be versatile enough to provide excellent task lighting when work is being done at the table and atmospheric lighting during dinner.

A question of style

Think about the style of dining furniture that is most appropriate for the room. The look will be determined by the cabinets, so don't introduce anything that jars with this. If you are tired of the cabinets themselves, it may not be necessary to rip them out. You could get a brand-new look by replacing the doors or simply sanding them down, painting them and replacing the handles. Changing the countertops or buying some chic

ABOVE: *The bay window of this kitchen holds a specially designed table and built-in banquette seating. The pillows create a comfortable back for the banquette and also help prevent draughts. For windows behind banquette seating, blinds such as these roman blinds (shades) are better than curtains.*

new appliances can have a dramatic effect, too, at a fraction of the cost of replacing the cabinets.

If you do plan to hold informal lunch or supper parties here, do not hold back on the table decoration. Plates, glasses, flatware and linen can all be used to good effect, just as if you were dressing the dining table. Chairs must be comfortable, with enough space between them that no one will feel crammed in. Serve spectacular dishes for maximum visual impact. Guests should not feel that eating in the kitchen is synonymous with inferior hospitality.

Floor plan: **Dining area**

Floor plan: Kitchen-dining area

Questionnaire: **Dining area**

Ask yourself the following questions about your dining area, and write the answers below. (Use a pencil so you can update it or change your mind.)

1 Who uses this room, and for what?

2 How suitable is it for these functions, and is the space adequate for your needs?

3 Would you prefer to have a larger dining table, and is there room for it?

4 Are any structural alterations needed?

5 Could the lighting be improved and, if so, how?

6 Are there enough electrical sockets (outlets) in the right places?

7 Does the architectural style detract from or add to the overall ambience?

8 What are the views like, both from inside to outside and through internal doorways?

9 What are the room's best features and how could these be accentuated?

10 What are its faults and are there any possible solutions?

11 Would it make the room more functional if radiators or air-conditioning units were moved?

12 Is there an existing feature that would make an eye-catching focal point? If so, how could it be dressed up to look really special?

13 Would the room benefit from having more than one focal point?

14 Do you have an idea for some other focal point you would like to introduce?

15 Is there enough storage for silver, china, glasses and linen? Would it be possible to fit in some more storage?

16 Is the room in need of redecoration?

17 Are there any colours/woods you cannot change (such as a marble fireplace or a mahogany mantelpiece) that will affect your scheme?

18 Will you need to replace the window treatments?

19 Do the flooring/carpet/rugs need to be replaced? Do you want to consider a different treatment?

20 Which furniture can you continue to use as it is, which can you use if you reupholster it, and what new furniture will you need?

21 Do you have a large enough serving area and somewhere to put food between courses?

22 If money were no object, how would you alter this room?

23 Would it be possible to do any of the 'dream' changes from the previous question?

24 What are your priorities, and how are you going to allocate the budget you are working within?

Job analysis: **Dining area**

surface	work to be done	materials and colours	comments
	DECORATION		
Ceiling			
paint			
Cornice (cove)			
paint			
Walls			
paint			
paper			
fabric			
Woodwork			
paint			
	STRUCTURAL ALTERATIONS		
Radiators			
type			
paint			
covers			
Electrics			
Plumbing			
radiators, if necessary			

Work Timetable: Dining area

job	supplier	start/completion dates	action required	job completed	comments
DECORATION					
Ceiling					
paint					
Cornice (cove)					
paint					
Walls					
paint					
paper					
fabric					
Woodwork					
paint					
STRUCTURAL ALTERATIONS					
Radiators					
type					
paint					
covers					
Electrics					
Plumbing					
radiators, if necessary					

Sourcing record: **Dining area**

Supplied by/manufacturer

Number of windows

Description: style, heading, length, material(s)

Main fabric: reference number, colour, width, pattern repeat

Main fabric: price per metre/yard, amount required, estimated cost

Edgings/trimmings (if any): description, reference number, colour, estimated cost

Lining (if any): description, reference number, colour, estimated cost

Interlining (if any): type, estimated cost

Tiebacks (if any): description, reference number, colour, estimated cost

Poles/rods, holdbacks, etc: description, reference number, colour, estimated cost

Estimated making and hanging cost

Total estimated cost

Comments

Sourcing record: **Dining area**

Supplied by/manufacturer

Description: material, suitability (light/normal/heavy domestic)

Reference number, colour, width

Price per square/linear metre/yard, amount required, estimated cost

Fitting/laying estimated cost, total estimated cost

Comments

Sourcing record: **Dining area**

Supplied by/manufacturer

Descriptions, reference numbers, colours

Price per light, number of lights, estimated cost

Installation estimated cost

Total estimated cost

Comments

Sourcing record: **Dining area**

Supplied by/manufacturer

___

Descriptions, reference numbers, colours

___

Wallcovering price per roll, amount required, estimated cost

___

Paint estimated cost

___

Labour estimated cost, total estimated cost

___

Comments

___

Sourcing record: **Dining area**

FURNITURE

Supplied by/manufacturer

___

Descriptions

___

Reference numbers, colours, sizes

___

Price per item

___

Total estimated cost

___

Comments

___

Sourcing record: **Dining area**

UPHOLSTERY

Supplied by/manufacturer

Descriptions: fabrics and trimmings

Reference numbers, colours, widths

Price per metre/yard, amount required, fabric estimated cost

Labour estimated cost, total estimated cost

Comments

Sourcing record: **Dining area**

ACCESSORIES

Supplied by/manufacturer

Descriptions

Reference numbers, colours

Price per item

Total estimated cost

Comments

Planning a study or library
With increasing numbers of people working from home for at least part of the time, a study has become essential in many homes. In fact, it is also an invaluable space for any number of other activities, from paying bills and doing the household accounts to writing letters or pursuing a hobby. Depending on how you want to use it, a study can be a room packed with files, work surfaces and high-tech equipment, or a small, cosy room with one or two comfortable chairs and a modest desk. A library, on the other hand, has a very specific use: the storage and enjoyment of books.

Making it functional
Often, of course, a room serves as both study and library. As always, your first decision when decorating this room, whatever its size, is to think about who will use it most and what they will use it for. Fill in the questionnaire at the end of this section (see page 104) to help with this process.

ABOVE: *Even the corner of a room may suffice to create a study area, especially if it has good natural light. Here, a chair upholstered in a magenta velvet picks up a colour in the glamorous printed silk used for the window treatment.*

ABOVE AND ABOVE RIGHT: *This small, square room is just big enough for a desk, a chair and a built-in bookcase which houses filing drawers below. The beautiful little inlaid desk, with its a lovely scroll front, goes perfectly with the chair, upholstered in a gaufrage mohair. The cup and saucer are from my Hearts range.*

Also as usual, plan the lighting right from the start. You obviously will need good task lighting for the desk or other work areas, being careful to avoid creating glare on any computer screens. However, you will get eyestrain unless you also have good background lighting. Finally, don't forget reading lamps next to armchairs or a sofa. Swing-arm 'library lights' are ideal.

Tip
A wall of books absorbs light, so good lighting is all the more important in a library.

When planning bookcases, make sure the shelving is strong enough to hold the books – nothing looks worse than sagging shelves. The sides should be a little thicker than the shelves themselves. I prefer bookcases to extend all the

ABOVE: *The study in my previous house was not somewhere to work as a family sitting room so much as a comfortable place to read. I chose dark woods and red tones because it was used more at night than by day.*

way to the ceiling, and I always have adjustable shelves. You can add interest by painting the insides of the bookcases in a contrasting colour.

The gentleman's club look

In many households, the study is a sanctuary from the hurly-burly of family life. If it does not double as a family sitting room, the chances are that it will acquire a masculine look, since a good-sized desk, a robust chair and ample storage are the essential requirements. Rather than trying to counteract this, you could make the masculine look the theme.

Elements of the look

There is a look for a study that is synonymous with English style and tradition: the 'gentleman's club' look. Think dark-panelled walls, a marble fireplace, book-lined shelves and sturdy furniture. It is a style so classic that it will simply never date,

ABOVE: *Everything blends in discreetly in this spacious library, from the leather-topped desk to the gilt-framed icon behind it. There is plenty of storage space in the floor-to-ceiling bookcases within the panelling.*

*Decorating trends come and go, but the
'gentleman's club' look endures, and nowhere
more than in the library.*

and it is replicated around the world, from Britain to New England to Hong Kong.

A room needs to have generous proportions if you are to recreate this look properly, and that can be a problem in modern houses and small apartments. Another challenge is combining modern technology with a style that has evolved over centuries. Electronic equipment is an essential requirement these days. Although this sort of study is not likely to be chosen by someone running a business from home, it may well be a secondary workplace or the control room from which the rest of the household is run. More often than not, a music system will also be required.

The secret is to install a wall of storage, which at first glance looks as if it only houses books. Have it custom-made to conceal all manner of

unsightly wires and equipment – cupboard doors or false books can then open out to reveal computer paraphernalia, a home entertainment centre, a security system or whatever else lies behind. Specialist paint techniques have become so sophisticated that it can be made to look as though it has been in the room for decades. Or, if you don't want a whole wall of storage, an armoire that has the back drilled to take cables will also effectively conceal a good deal of electronic equipment.

Adding interest and comfort

Sombre colours, rich wood panelling and pools of soft light are part of this decorating approach. However, you can introduce colour and pattern through upholstery, the window treatment or a rug, to punctuate the dark surroundings. Books and other publications inject interest, as do favourite paintings, photographs and other personal possessions.

This can be the perfect place to display collections, which might well provide the starting point for your scheme. Choose a background colour that will show them to best advantage and light them well. Items that can be wall-mounted are an excellent alternative to paintings.

Although the desk is probably central to the room – the focal point, in effect – it is important to include an inviting seating area as well. The atmosphere should be dignified and restrained but also superbly comfortable.

LEFT: *The side chairs in the library that is pictured on page 101 have cushions in a green and gold weave piped and buttoned in gold, echoing the gilding on the desk and picture frames.*

Floor plan: **Study/library**

Questionnaire: **Study/library**

Ask yourself the following questions about the room that serves as a study or library, and write the answers below. (Use a pencil so you can update it or change your mind.)

1 Who uses this room, and for what?

_____

_____

_____

2 How suitable is it for these functions, and is the space adequate for your needs?

_____

_____

3 Are any structural alterations needed?

_____

_____

4 Could the lighting be improved and, if so, how?

_____

_____

_____

5 Are there enough electrical sockets (outlets) in the right places?

_____

6 Does the architectural style detract from or add to the overall ambience?

_____

_____

7 Would it make the room more functional if radiators or air-conditioning units were moved?

_____

_____

8 Would it be possible to fit in some more storage?

_____

_____

9 Is the room in need of redecoration?

_____

_____

_____

10 Will you need to replace the window treatments?

_____

_____

11 Do the flooring/carpet/rugs need to be replaced? Do you want to consider a different treatment?

_____

_____

12 Do you have work surfaces?

_____

_____

13 Which furniture can you continue to use as it is, which can you use if you reupholster it, and what new furniture will you need?

_____

_____

14 If money were no object, how would you alter this room?

_____

_____

15 Would it be possible to do any of the 'dream' changes from the previous question?

_____

_____

16 What are your priorities, and how are you going to allocate the budget you are working within?

_____

_____

_____

Job analysis: **Study/library**

surface	work to be done	materials and colours	comments
	DECORATION		
Ceiling			
paint			
Cornice (cove)			
paint			
Walls			
paint			
paper			
fabric			
Woodwork			
paint			
	STRUCTURAL ALTERATIONS		
Radiators			
type			
paint			
covers			
Electrics			
Plumbing			
radiators, if necessary			

Work Timetable: **Study/library**

job	supplier	start/completion dates	action required	job completed	comments
		DECORATION			
Ceiling					
paint					
Cornice (cove)					
paint					
Walls					
paint					
paper					
fabric					
Woodwork					
paint					
		STRUCTURAL ALTERATIONS			
Radiators					
type					
paint					
covers					
Electrics					
Plumbing					
radiators, if necessary					

Sourcing record: **Study/library**

Supplied by/manufacturer

___

Number of windows

___

Description: style, heading, length, material(s)

___

Main fabric: reference number, colour, width, pattern repeat

___

Main fabric: price per metre/yard, amount required, estimated cost

___

Edgings/trimmings (if any): description, reference number, colour, estimated cost

___

Lining (if any): description, reference number, colour, estimated cost

___

Interlining (if any): type, estimated cost

___

Tiebacks (if any): description, reference number, colour, estimated cost

___

Poles/rods, holdbacks, etc: description, reference number, colour, estimated cost

___

Estimated making and hanging cost

___

Total estimated cost

___

Comments

___

Sourcing record: **Study/library**

FLOORING

Supplied by/manufacturer

Description: material, suitability (light/normal/heavy domestic)

Reference number, colour, width

Price per square/linear metre/yard, amount required, estimated cost

Fitting/laying estimated cost, total estimated cost

Comments

Sourcing record: **Study/library**

LIGHTING

Supplied by/manufacturer

Descriptions, reference numbers, colours

Price per light, number of lights, estimated cost

Installation estimated cost

Total estimated cost

Comments

Sourcing record: **Study/library**

Supplied by/manufacturer

Descriptions, reference numbers, colours

Wallcovering price per roll, amount required, estimated cost

Paint estimated cost

Labour estimated cost, total estimated cost

Comments

Sourcing record: **Study/library**

FURNITURE

Supplied by/manufacturer

Descriptions

Reference numbers, colours, sizes

Price per item

Total estimated cost

Comments

Sourcing record: **Study/library**

UPHOLSTERY

Supplied by/manufacturer

_____

Descriptions: fabrics and trimmings

_____

Reference numbers, colours, widths

_____

Price per metre/yard, amount required, fabric estimated cost

_____

Labour estimated cost, total estimated cost

_____

Comments

_____

_____

Sourcing record: **Study/library**

ACCESSORIES

Supplied by/manufacturer

_____

Descriptions

_____

Reference numbers, colours

_____

Price per item

_____

Total estimated cost

_____

Comments

_____

_____

Bedroom essentials

Your bedroom is the most personal room within your home. It should offer you sanctuary from the day's cares – an oasis of calm in which you can feel rejuvenated and soothed. Bedrooms are much more than places in which to sleep, and you need to design your bedroom with this in mind.

Bedlinen is one of life's simpler luxuries, and a bed should look as comfortable as it feels.

Where comfort reigns supreme

If you can find space for a small sitting area in the bedroom, then you need to apply the same rules as you would to a conventional sitting room; chairs should be comfortably upholstered, and there should be surfaces at hand for cups or books. Rather than settling for fabrics that echo those of the bed, choose ones that have different but harmonizing patterns or tones, in order to set the sitting area apart a little.

ABOVE: *Even in a small bedroom, aim to fit in elements that are important to you, such as a comfortable bed, good reading lights and storage for books.*

The key to creating a bedroom where you feel cocooned from life's cares is to surround yourself with things you consider essential to quality of life. If you love to read in bed, for example, it makes sense to have floor-to-ceiling shelves at each side of the bed filled with much-loved books.

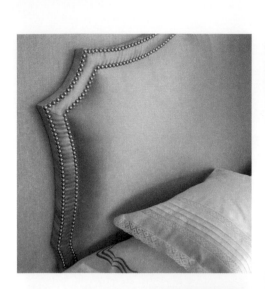

You must also have a well-positioned light to read by; adjustable swing-arm lights positioned over the headboard are ideal.

If the bedroom is where you like to indulge yourself with facials or manicures, then a dressing table is a priority (see page 121). And, of course, having enough clothes storage is a primary consideration because without it you will always find yourself living in chaos.

The bed itself must be superbly comfortable and should also look inviting. Fine-quality bedlinen is not a frivolous buy but the kind of luxury that, once you have bought it, you wonder how you ever managed without. A headboard that

TOP LEFT, TOP RIGHT, ABOVE LEFT AND ABOVE: *Essentials for a comfortable bedroom include a supportive headboard, such as the one at top left upholstered in a pale grey satin and close-nailed, and good lighting. The bedroom at top right has both a table lamp for ambient lighting and an adjustable, swing-arm light for reading. An armchair (above left) and personal photos and mementos (above) help make the room a haven.*

supports the back comfortably when you sit up in bed is also a must. Bedrooms are, above all, sensuous places, so indulge yourself as much as possible, whether it is with flowers, scented candles or fine fabrics.

The traditional bedroom

For many people, a four-poster bed is the height of elegance and romance, but if you are planning to have one, remember that it must be done well or not at all. Four-posters can look stylish and modern without any hangings, or with just a canopy or narrow, non-functioning curtains. However, if you do want to have a full set of four-poster hangings, bear in mind that they use vast quantities of fabric. And, of course, it is perfectly possible to have an elegant, traditional bedroom without a four-poster at all.

The over-scaled bed

Don't be deterred if your bedroom has fairly modest proportions and a ceiling of only average height. A 120cm- (4ft-) wide four-poster may still fit in, and it is also possible to buy custom-made four-posters. The over-scaled bed will make a room appear larger than it is, rather than smaller, because it will trick the eye, making you subconsciously believe that the bedroom must be large if such a bed fits in it.

You also need to think carefully about the backdrop you are going to give such a strong focal point. Plain walls are fine for a contemporary look, but glorious beds demand a more decorative

ABOVE: *In my bedroom the walls are covered in a pale pink linen, accented with Dior grey. On the folding doors to the bathroom I have used antiqued mirror glass.*

setting. Pattern is a wonderful design ingredient, which happily is making a comeback, and the bedroom is the perfect place in which to use it because it injects a feeling of warmth and cosiness. However, it is important to offset it with solid colours as well, as the eye will become tired if the effect is too riotous.

This is one of the reasons why chair rails are so effective – they provide a visual break and the opportunity to introduce a solid-coloured area

Classic style should always be combined with comfort, and prettiness with practicality.

adjacent to a patterned one. Adding a chair rail is also one of the most immediate ways of giving a modern apartment a classic look.

Furnishing in classic style

To maintain this traditional style throughout the room, aim for symmetry. A pair of tables or chests with large lamps flanking the bed is both practical and aesthetically pleasing. Or you could opt for a chest on one side and a table on the other, so long as they are of the same height, allowing the lamps to be in line. If you have room, a piece of furniture at the foot of the bed – such as a chaise, a chest or a stool – will emphasize the feeling of grandeur, as well as providing a convenient surface on which to rest a breakfast tray.

ABOVE LEFT, ABOVE AND OPPOSITE: *An elegant French daybed look is a good way to create a classic look in a room that is too small for a four-poster. Using matching fabric and wallpaper disguises the room's awkward proportions.*

If you want to achieve a feeling of elegance, introduce furniture that would be as at home in the living room as in the bedroom. A bookcase or writing bureau will look as fitting as a dressing table or wardrobe, and will help the bedroom double as an extra sitting room by day, as will comfortable armchairs.

Lamps, pictures and books give a homey feeling. Don't forget family photographs, favourite ornaments, much-loved heirlooms – these all play their part in achieving that final look.

Lavishly layered
The decorated look is the antidote to minimalism. It requires the designer to introduce layer upon layer into a room, building up a look that appears to have been in place for ever.

The principal pattern

First find your starting point. For me, this is usually a fabric because it is through colour and pattern that I set the style of the room; the luxurious quality of soft furnishings is pivotal to the success of a scheme. If there is a matching wallpaper available, so much the better. Using one bold pattern for walls, windows and upholstery is a way of bringing an immediate signature into a room, giving it character and interest.

Be lavish with whatever material you choose. Better to use reams of something inexpensive than to cut corners with the fabric you long to use. Perhaps you can't afford to make curtains with

BELOW AND OPPOSITE: *The colours of the chocolate-brown grass paper and blue and white Parsua rug are brought together in the lovely old chintz used for this window treatment. Including vintage elements gives a room layers and a sense of history.*

Think of the bold pattern as the diva of your scheme, while the coordinating fabrics are the chorus.

your number one choice, but could use it to upholster a stool instead. Try not to be led by fashion too much when making your decision. This is a look that transcends current fads and is designed to withstand the passing of time. Think of English country houses with bedrooms that have not changed for years – the idea is to create something equally enduring in your own home.

Coordinating fabrics

Fabrics that coordinate will add another layer of interest to the look. Stripes, trellises or sprigs are ideal choices, as they add variety without being overwhelming. Even using them just for lining or piping can be very effective. Think too about the colour of linings; a glimpse of another colour can be tantalizing to the eye.

Another approach is to use the main pattern on the walls, headboard, bed skirt and curtains while keeping everything else – carpet, chairs, bedside tables, bedcover or duvet, and lampshades – in a solid colour that appears in the pattern. Carpets should be chosen to coordinate, rather than to dominate. You need not be limited to solid colours – textured cut-and-loop designs are an excellent halfway house between solid colours and patterned.

All the trimmings

Having decided on the big canvas, you can think about the details. Every bedroom needs an element of fun and a dash of individuality. I am a big fan of braids, bobbles and beads, which are great ways to finish off fabrics, tie back curtains

ABOVE: *This pretty room has comfort at its heart. The use of the same fabric on the upholstered headboard and the bed skirt as on the walls creates a spacious feel, making the bed less dominant.*

and add detail to any room. I often use rope in the corners to delineate where one wall meets another. Trims can match the fabric, be in a harmonious colour or contrast with it, depending on how dramatic an effect you want.

Accessories such as lampshades and pillows bring another layer of interest into the room, subtly lifting it a notch. When the room is finished, assess it from all angles. Rooms often need a final tweak, though it might simply be a matter of adding flowers, straightening pictures or plumping up pillows.

Private spaces

Your bedroom is not just a treasured sanctuary but also the place where you prepare the face you present to the world. This means having space in which to pamper yourself – a private corner that is yours alone.

The dressing table

For most women, that private corner is the dressing table. It need not be a conventional design: writing bureaux, side tables or chests of drawers can be commandeered for use if necessary.

ABOVE: *Traditional dressing tables like this antique one are enjoying a revival and can be very beautiful. If you are lucky enough to have an old one, you could transform it by giving it a new skirt.*

LEFT: *This pretty bedside table, though small, holds the essentials and is exactly the right height. Fabric and framed pictures disguise the jib door behind it.*

have a separate dressing room or bathroom, it might be better to give them a private corner of their own in there.

Nightstands

Good storage is the key to keeping bedrooms calm and serene. This applies not only to clothes, but to each area within the room, especially nightstands, which should be kept as free from the flotsam and jetsam of daily life as possible. Choose the largest you have room for, so that you have space for a lamp, books, a telephone, radio, clock, tissues, water – and flowers.

Dressing rooms

One of today's greatest luxuries is to have a dressing room off the master bedroom. By removing all the paraphernalia associated with clothes from the bedroom, you create quite a different atmosphere there: it is much more likely to become the calm oasis you long for. The dressing room, by contrast, is a busy place devoted solely to function. It is the equivalent of the utility room adjacent to the kitchen.

A dressing room requires very little except adequate clothes storage, good lighting, a generous-sized mirror and a chair. When designing your own, take a hard look at the clothes you need to store, and work out exactly how much hanging and folding space you need. Custom-built closets make sense here, to make maximum use of available space. The interior should offer a comprehensive range of drawers, adjustable rails, hooks, shoe racks and perhaps a fold-out ironing board. Cubbyholes for bags, shoes and belts are

Tip
Instead of bedside tables, use small chests of drawers if you have space, as they provide a bigger tabletop as well as storage underneath.

The essentials are a good-sized mirror and a generous surface on which to keep beauty products. Ideally, it should be placed near a window, but artificial lighting is also necessary to boost dull mornings or for use by night. You will need a chair or stool, too, but if space is tight you could push it against a wall when not in use.

A simple vase of flowers on the dressing table is lovely to focus on when you wake up. However, the most important thing is to make clear to other members of the family that the dressing table is your own domain – not an additional surface on which they can throw down keys, spare change or old receipts. Men do need the equivalent of a dressing table surface if they are to respect this. It need not be in the bedroom: if you

ABOVE AND LEFT: *A walk-in closet is a wonderful asset –
it means that the bedroom can remain the calming,
tranquil space it should be. It also provides somewhere to
store shoes properly, even if it means buying fifty sets of
matching linen shoe trees.*

also an asset. Do not forget to allow for all those
awkwardly shaped or bulky items, such as large
hats or boots.

Some kind of labelling system might also be
advisable. If you have an impressively large shoe
collection, for example, all stored within their
boxes, take photos of each one and glue them to
the boxes. This way you will not have to waste
time rummaging through them all trying to find
the right pair.

Guest rooms

There is more to having people to stay than simply providing a bed for the night. You want guests to leave your home feeling relaxed and well looked after, warmly anticipating their next visit. A lot of this will depend on the room itself. Often, guest rooms double as something else – a study or hobby room, perhaps. This might be essential given the size of your house, but when other people come to stay, it should be their home, too. That means any other activities that take place here should be tucked well out of sight.

Making guests feel at home

The next consideration is how much storage you have provided for your guests' use: not just space in which to hang or fold clothes but also an area for shoes, luggage and the like. People need to unpack in order to feel properly comfortable, and it is disheartening for them to open each drawer and find it already full to bursting point.

Guests need a comfortable, generously proportioned bed, high-quality bedlinen and plenty of pillows. There must also be a full-length mirror and, if at all possible, a couple of chairs and a lamp so that they won't have to sit on the bed when reading or chatting in their room. Finally, bring in as many homey touches as possible, such as books and magazines, photographs, flowers, water carafes or bottles of mineral water, and drinking glasses.

BELOW: *My guest room is small but restful, light and airy. I believe that there is nothing more welcoming than top-of-the-range linen.*

It is not fair to expect guests to negotiate an exercise bike, artist's easel or computer work station in order to get to bed.

Bathrooms and cloakrooms
Bathrooms that are separate from the other rooms have a different character to those linked directly to a bedroom, where you have to consider the flow from one area into the next. The priority in any bathroom or cloakroom (powder room), however, is to create a warm, safe haven with the best plumbing possible.

Back to basics

As with every other room you are redecorating, think about whether the layout is as efficient as it could be. For example, if you are tall and have a small bath, consider changing the layout in order to accommodate a generous-sized tub that you will really enjoy. If that can't be done, perhaps you should think about ripping the bath out completely and replacing it with an invigorating and energizing power shower. If the bathroom is shared and more than one person needs to use the sink at the same time every morning, you could install two sinks.

If you are starting from scratch, it is always best to choose white bathroom fixtures – other colours are too subject to the whims of fashion.

ABOVE LEFT AND ABOVE: *The black and gold extravaganza that is my guest cloakroom (powder room). It is a tiny, dark, misshapen room under the eaves, so I have used this wallpaper to make it darker, richer and more glittery, while disguising the uneven contours.*

Just think about the scorn with which some of the colours that have been fashionable in the past are regarded now. However, that does not mean you have to keep to neutrals throughout. Floors, walls, window treatments, rugs, towels and bath accessories all give plenty of opportunity for injecting colour and texture.

Hard floors are still most people's preference for the bathroom because, in an area devoted to water, they are regarded as more hygienic.

If the result is too masculine for your own taste, look for ways of softening the effect slightly – perhaps through window treatments or by introducing a piece of furniture usually found elsewhere in the house.

Streamlined sophistication

Many people desire bathrooms that are much harder-edged than the rest of the house. Materials such as marble are popular because they withstand water and steam, while imprinting a

LEFT AND BELOW: *Two versions of traditional style: the small shower room (left) is classically styled, crisp and fresh, while the large bathroom (below) incorporates chintz and wood to avoid a clinical look.*

LEFT AND BELOW: *Two takes on the vanity unit: the mirrored cabinet (left) has been custom-made and has a Venetian mirror above it, while the rustic cabinet (below) is painted tongue-and-groove wood and is combined with a simple modern mirror and wooden shutters.*

signature of luxury. However, a bathroom that is covered totally in any hard, reflective surface, be it marble, another type of stone or tiles, often looks rather cool and austere. Instead, think about combining materials that each bring different qualities to an interior. Wood and stone, for example, work well together – wood introduces a mellow, warm tone, while stone defines the contours of a space.

Because the bathroom is primarily a functional room, it lends itself to built-in furniture in much the same way as the kitchen does. Such furniture should follow the shape of the room as much as possible, so that there are no ugly gaps or sharp edges. Sinks that are inset into a countertop also follow this precept and are aesthetically pleasing.

Sensual softness

Increasing numbers of people prefer to decorate their bathrooms much as they would other rooms of the house. That means fabrics, free-standing furniture, paintings and accessories. Naturally, practicalities have to be tackled first. For example, steam is a destructive element, so you must have

good ventilation in place. Lighting, too, must be considered, not just on a functional level but in terms of the ambience it creates. Make sure your choices comply with health and safety regulations.

In my own bathrooms I prefer a look that is best described as classic with a twist. Sterile white tiles do not have the same appeal for me as warm colours and elegant materials. My master bathroom (see pages 128–9) has pale pink lacquer walls that exactly match the linen-covered walls of the adjacent bedroom (see page 115). A sink is inset into a 1930s buffet that we silverleafed and then glazed. Introducing architectural features, such as a chair rail and cornice, and covering the walls with black-and-white and sepia pictures of my children are other tricks I employ.

The joy of bathrooms such as this is that they express the owner's personality. The focus is not so much on the bath itself as on the decorative

*I like a bathroom that has the ambience
of a sitting room, rather than that of a hospital.*

ideas and items that surround it. This approach also promotes the idea of indulgence, which is a seductive notion in the bathroom. These are not rooms to hurry through between waking and dressing, but places in which to unwind and soothe away the anxieties of the day.

OPPOSITE AND ABOVE: *My bathroom is a delight of mirrors and is lit from a skylight, so the quality of light is always good. We adapted the 1930s buffet to accommodate the plumbing for the sink. A piece of furniture can often be adapted to house a sink, and this one worked well, as it offered so much storage space.*

Floor plan: **Bedroom**

Floor plan: **Bathroom**

Questionnaire: **Bedroom**

Ask yourself the following questions about your bedroom, and write the answers below. (Use a pencil so you can update it or change your mind.)

1 Who uses this room? Is it used for any other purposes such as a home gym, home office or sitting room?

2 How suitable is it for these functions, and is the space adequate for your needs?

3 Are any structural alterations needed?

4 Could the lighting be improved and, if so, how?

5 Are there enough electrical sockets (outlets) in the right places?

6 Does the architectural style detract from or add to the overall ambience?

7 What are the room's best features and how could these be accentuated?

8 What are its faults and are there any possible solutions?

9 Would it make the room more functional if radiators or air-conditioning units were moved?

10 Is the bed an eye-catching focal point? Could it be dressed up to look really special or would you want to replace the bed itself? Is it the right size?

11 Would the bedroom benefit from having an additional focal point? If so, what could it be?

12 Would it be possible to fit in some more storage?

13 Is the room in need of redecoration?

14 Are there any colours/woods you cannot change (such as a marble fireplace or a mahogany mantelpiece) that will affect your scheme?

15 Will you need to replace the window treatments?

16 Do the flooring/carpet/rugs need to be replaced? Do you want to consider a different treatment?

17 Which furniture can you continue to use as it is, and what new furniture will you need?

18 Do you have a dressing table? If so, could you make it more attractive and useful? If not, is there somewhere you could put one, or an existing piece of furniture you could adapt?

19 Do you have a seating area? If not, is there somewhere you could fit one in?

20 If money were no object, how would you alter this room?

21 Would it be possible to do any of the 'dream' changes from the previous question?

22 What are your priorities, and how are you going to allocate the budget you are working within?

Questionnaire: Bathroom

Ask yourself the following questions about your bathroom, and write the answers below. (Use a pencil so you can update it or change your mind.)

1   Who uses this bathroom and at what time of day is it most used?

_____

_____

2   Are the space and layout adequate for your needs?

_____

_____

3   Are any structural alterations needed?

_____

_____

4   Could the lighting and ventilation be improved and, if so, how?

_____

_____

5   Does the architectural style detract from or add to the overall ambience?

_____

6   What are the room's best features and how could these be accentuated?

_____

_____

7   What are its faults and are there any possible solutions?

_____

_____

_____

8   Do the fittings need replacing? If so, is it worth considering rearranging them to make the layout work better?

_____

_____

_____

9 Would you want to replace a shower with a bath/shower, a bath with a large shower, and/or one sink with two?

_____

_____

10 Would it make the room more functional if radiators or air-conditioning units were moved?

_____

_____

11 Would it be possible to fit in some more storage?

_____

_____

12 Is the room in need of retiling or redecoration?

_____

_____

13 Are there any colours/woods you cannot change (such as fittings or tiles) that will affect your scheme?

_____

_____

_____

14 Will you need to replace the window treatments?

_____

_____

15 Does the flooring need to be replaced? Do you want to consider a different treatment?

_____

_____

16 If money were no object, how would you alter this room?

_____

_____

17 Would it be possible to do any of the 'dream' changes from the previous question?

_____

_____

_____

18 What are your priorities, and how are you going to allocate the budget you are working within?

_____

_____

Job analysis: **Bedroom**

surface	work to be done	materials and colours	comments
	DECORATION		
Ceiling			
paint			
Cornice (cove)			
paint			
Walls			
paint			
paper			
fabric			
Woodwork			
paint			
	STRUCTURAL ALTERATIONS		
Radiators			
type			
paint			
covers			
Electrics			
Plumbing			
radiators, if necessary			

Work Timetable: **Bedroom**

job	supplier	start/completion dates	action required	job completed	comments
	DECORATION				
Ceiling					
paint					
Cornice (cove)					
paint					
Walls					
paint					
paper					
fabric					
Woodwork					
paint					
	STRUCTURAL ALTERATIONS				
Radiators					
type					
paint					
covers					
Electrics					
Plumbing					
radiators, if necessary					

Job analysis: **Bathroom**

surface	work to be done	materials and colours	comments
	DECORATION		
Ceiling			
paint			
Cornice (cove)			
paint			
Walls			
paint			
paper			
fabric			
Woodwork			
paint			
	STRUCTURAL ALTERATIONS		
Radiators			
type			
paint			
covers			
Electrics			
Plumbing			
radiators, if necessary			

Work Timetable: **Bathroom**

job	supplier	start/completion dates	action required	job completed	comments
		DECORATION			
Ceiling					
paint					
Cornice (cove)					
paint					
Walls					
paint					
paper					
fabric					
Woodwork					
paint					
		STRUCTURAL ALTERATIONS			
Radiators					
type					
paint					
covers					
Electrics					
Plumbing					
radiators, if necessary					

Sourcing record: **Bedroom and bathroom**

WINDOW TREATMENTS

Supplied by/manufacturer

Number of windows

Description: style, heading, length, material(s)

Main fabric: reference number, colour, width, pattern repeat

Main fabric: price per metre/yard, amount required, estimated cost

Edgings/trimmings (if any): description, reference number, colour, estimated cost

Lining (if any): description, reference number, colour, estimated cost

Interlining (if any): type, estimated cost

Tiebacks (if any): description, reference number, colour, estimated cost

Poles/rods, holdbacks, etc: description, reference number, colour, estimated cost

Estimated making and hanging cost

Total estimated cost

Comments

Sourcing record: **Bedroom and bathroom**

FLOORING/TILES

Supplied by/manufacturer

Description: material, suitability (light/normal/heavy domestic)

Reference numbers, colours, width, tile size and thickness

Price per square/linear metre/yard, amount required, estimated cost

Fitting/laying estimated cost, total estimated cost

Comments

Sourcing record: **Bedroom and bathroom**

LIGHTING

Supplied by/manufacturer

Descriptions, reference numbers, colours

Price per light, number of lights, estimated cost

Installation estimated cost

Total estimated cost

Comments

Sourcing record: **Bedroom and bathroom**

Supplied by/manufacturer

_____

Descriptions, reference numbers, colours

_____

Wallcovering price per roll, amount required, estimated cost

_____

Paint estimated cost

_____

Labour estimated cost, total estimated cost

_____

Comments

_____

_____

Sourcing record: **Bedroom and bathroom**

Supplied by/manufacturer

_____

Descriptions

_____

Reference numbers, colours, sizes

_____

Price per item

_____

Total estimated cost

_____

Comments

_____

_____

Sourcing record: **Bedroom and bathroom**

UPHOLSTERY

Supplied by/manufacturer

Descriptions: fabrics and trimmings

Reference numbers, colours, widths

Price per metre/yard, amount required, fabric estimated cost

Labour estimated cost, total estimated cost

Comments

Sourcing record: **Bedroom and bathroom**

ACCESSORIES

Supplied by/manufacturer

Descriptions

Reference numbers, colours

Price per item

Total estimated cost

Comments

distributors

Nina Campbell Furniture Distributed by
ARTHUR BRETT & SONS LTD

UK & Europe Head Office
Tel: +44 (0)1603 480725
Fax: + 44 (0)1603 788984
USA Head Office
Tel: + 1 (0)336 886 7102
Fax: +1 (0)336 886 7078

LAMBSWOOL THROWS
Distributed by JOHNSTONS
UK & Europe Head Office
Tel: +44 (0)1343 554000
Fax: +44 (0)1343 554055
USA Distributor
Tel: 800 544 5966
Fax: 336 887 3334

WALL TO WALL CARPETS
Distributed by WOOL CLASSICS
UK & Europe Head Office
Tel: +44 (0)20 7349 0090
Distributed by SAXONY
USA Distributor
Tel: +1 (0)212 755 7100

NINA CAMPBELL HOME FRAGRANCE
Distributed by HOME 360
UK & Europe Office
Tel: +44 (0)20 7491 8877
Fax: +44 (0)20 7491 8878
USA Head Office
Tel: +1 (0)713 344 1665
Fax: +1 (0)713 344 1784

NINA CAMPBELL LINENS
Wholesale contact FIONA MCKELVIE
Tel: +44 (0)20 8488 5984
Fax: +44 (0)20 8488 5984

Nina Campbell's fabric and wallpaper collections are distributed throughout the world by **OSBORNE & LITTLE**

Visit: www.osborneandlittle.com for stockists and details of agents' showrooms.
Email oandl@osborneandlittle.com

UK
UK Head Office
(For general enquiries)
OSBORNE & LITTLE
Riverside House
26 Osiers Road
London SW18 1NH
Tel: +44 (0)20 8812 3000

UK Showroom
(Open to the trade and public)
OSBORNE & LITTLE
304 King's Road
London SW3 5UH
Tel: +44 (0)20 7352 1456

USA
USA Head Office
(For general enquiries)
OSBORNE & LITTLE INC.
90 Commerce Road
Stamford, CT 06902
Tel: +1 (0)203 359500